One Foot on the Mountain

AN ANTHOLOGY OF BRITISH FEMINIST POETRY 1969-1979

EDITED BY LILIAN MOHIN

Published by Onlywomen Press Ltd.,
38, Mount Pleasant, London WC1.

Second printing 1980
Third printing 1982
Fourth printing 1984
Photographs in this reprint differ in some cases from those appearing in the
original.

ISBN 0 906500 01 X

Typesetting by Dark Moon
Layout by Lilian Mohin
Title from "Love Song" by Alison Fell

Cover design by Deborah Stern

Printed in Great Britain by
Redwood Burn Ltd., Trowbridge, Wiltshire, and
bound by Pegasus Bookbinding, Melksham, Wiltshire.

Onlywomen Press believes it is necessary to create a women's communication
system. At the very least, this would mean we could and would print our own
books on our own machines with our own hands. At present, we have machines
which are so old and small that if we had printed this book on them the con-
sequent binding costs would have priced this anthology out of existence. Our
machines are adequate for the smaller jobs (leaflets, pamphlets, posters) which
we are continuing to print for other groups. We are in the process of acquiring
improved equipment as one more step towards the realisation of our aims as
feminist publishers and printers. We welcome your support.

Onlywomen Press gratefully acknowledges that this book has been published
with financial assistance from the Arts Council of Great Britain and from the
Greater London Arts Association.

"It can create the rage, the longing, the joy, the courage, the consciousness to make real revolution. For poetry is a dangerous force; it can move mountains; wars have been made over it . . . When people have been robbed of their own culture and forced to identify with the oppressor's culture, there is no real way they can make a revolution, unless of course they use *his* means and *his* weapons and wind up like *him*. But, when contrarily, people begin to create or regain their *own* culture, there is no stopping them."

Robin Morgan*

* "poetry and women's culture",
The New Women's Survival Sourcebook
(Alfred A. Knopf, New York, 1975) p.109.

ACKNOWLEDGEMENTS

Copyright © of the poems in this volume belongs to the authors unless otherwise acknowledged below.

Alison Fell — "Women in the Cold War" appeared first in *Cutlasses and Earrings*, (Playbooks 2, London 1977). "For Maria Burke", "Love Song", "Atlanta Streets", and "Girl's Gifts" appeared first in *Licking the Bed Clean*, (Teeth Imprints, London, 1978)

Ann Oosthuizen — "Bulletins from the Front Line" and "I do not remember you with pleasure" first appeared in *Licking the Bed Clean*, (Teeth Imprints, London, 1978)

Astra — "gift giving"and "coming out celibate" first appeared in *Seven Women*, (Women's Literature Collective, London, 1976).

Caroline Gilfillan — "lesbian play on T.V.", and "you have put out my one eye" first appeared in *Seven Women*, (Women's Literature Collective, London, 1976)

Chandra Masoliver — "I am alone when" first appeared in *Seven Women*, (Women's Literature Collective, London, 1976)."oh the fragments of the rain", "I have felt myself not loved" and "the pressures of a sea change" first appeared in *too late for ignorance*, (Women's Literature Collective, London, 1974)

Diana Scott — "Of The Children of Other People" and "Love Poem to Myself" first appeared in *If Women want to Speak, What Language Do They Use?* (Beyond Patriarchy Publications, London, 1977). "Poem for the Dark Goddess: on the full moon" first appeared in *The Politics of Matriarchy*, (Matriarchy Study Group Publications, London, 1979)

Harriet Rose — "The Lost Princess' first appeared in *Iron.*

Janet Dube — "it'll take a long time" and "brief for a statement to the authorities' first appeared in *it'll take a long time*, (Onlywomen Press when it was called Women's Press, London, 1976)

Judith Barrington — "Where are the brave new worlds" first appeared in *Deviation*, (Onlywomen Press when it was called Women's Press, London, 1976)

Judith Carey — "The family man's hands are cold" and "Pompous in Pinstripe" first appeared in the *Cambridge Women's liberation Newsletter*, December, 1978

Judith Kazantzis — "The Bath" first appeared in *Spare Rib*. "To J" first appeared in *minefield*, (Sidgwick & Jackson, London 1977)

Lilian Mohin — "sleep/power" first appeared in *CRACKS*, (Onlywomen Press when it was called Women's Press, London 1976). "Too late for ignorance" first appeared in the pamphlet of the same title (Women's Literature Collective, London, 1974). "this dream recurs", first appeared in *Seven Women* (Women's Literature Collective, London, 1976)

Margaret de V. Wills — "Badger", "Emergency Ward New Years Eve", "It", "Astarte in Green Shawl" first appeared in *Badger*, (Pat Van Twest & Hilary Thompson, Bristol, 1973)

Mary Coghill — "The is the Moment: Then" and "Goddess Creation" first appeared in *If Women Want To Speak, What Language Do They Use?*, (Beyond Patriarchy Publications, London, 1977)

Mary Michaels — "evening" first appeared in *Spare Rib*

Michelene Wandor — "Birth", "London airport", and "Some Male Poets" first appeared in *Cutlasses and Earrings*, (Playbooks 2, London, 1977). "June 1974" first appeared in *Spare Rib*. "The occasional moment" first appeared in *Red Rag*. "Pin Money" was written as part of *Floorshow*, a theatre piece staged by Monstrous Regiment.

Michele Roberts — "I have been wanting to mourn" first appeared in *Licking the Bed Clean*, (Teeth Imprints, London, 1978)

Pauling Long — "If Women Could Speak, What Language Would They Choose" first appeared in *If Women Want To Speak, What Language Do They Use?*, (Beyond Patriarchy Publications, London, 1977)

Sally Berry — "I scream", "I knew the quicksand was there", "It was more", "By a thread", and "I have pretended" all first appeared in *Seven Women*, (Women's Literature Collective, London, 1976)

Sheila Rowbotham — "253 bus", "The sad tale of nobody me", and "The role of women in the Revolution" first appeared in *Cutlasses and Earrings*, (Playbooks 2, London, 1977)

Sheila Shulman — "Poem for Jackie" first appeared in *Too late for ignorance*, (Women's Literature Collective, London, 1974). "now as I begin to age" first appeared in *Seven Women*, (Women's Literature Collective, London, 1976)

Stef Pixner — all the poems in this anthology by Stef Pixner first appeared in *Licking the Bed Clean*, (Teeth Imprints, London, 1978)

Valerie Sinason — "There once was a woman" first appeared in *Contemporary Women Poets*, (Rondo Publications, Liverpool, 1975).

for Hilda, my mother

CONTENTS

The poets are arranged alphabetically by first name.

INTRODUCTION

In the last decade, the Women's Liberation Movement has shown us that it is necessary to redefine just about everything. Slowly we are beginning to do precisely that. Consciousness raising groups, the basic stuff of Women's Liberation, have been putting flesh on the bones of the idea that the personal is political, that our individual experiences have social significance, are important on a world political scale. Feminist poets are carrying this decision to tell new truths about ourselves and the world into a public arena. The conceptual restrictions of what it is appropriate for women to be, to think, to write are being carefully eroded and we are creating a new and entire way of perceiving. We can only remove the enormous morass of patriarchal concepts encompassing, impregnating, surrounding, bearing down on us through this piecing together of new ways of thinking.

Poetry, with its tradition of concentrated insights, its brevity of form, is an ideal vehicle for the kind of politics we propose. In Britain, the Women's Liberation Movement has thrown up many pamphlets, papers, poems, few long sustained prose works. The nature of most women's lives, of course, makes any written work more likely to come out in a short form, as we snatch moments from what we are supposed to be doing as mothers, as wives, as workers at the bottom of the heap. Poetry has traditionally been the place to state condensed and particular perceptions which elsewhere would be called mad or perhaps banal. To describe the ordinary fabric of our lives and to say these things are significant has always been an element in poetry. The intimate perception can quickly (with a kind of shorthand achieved by metaphor or economical phrasing) be seen to be deep, new, illuminating. I think that these are some of the reasons why many feminists have chosen to write poetry. But we have begun to do really new work, feminist work, with this form and, by doing so, are redefining poetry as well.

Because men have defined both poetry and politics differently than we do, creating a separation between them, there exist in "literature" few poems called political. Those there are have often been labelled propaganda as a way of saying that they're no good. These were usually poems about the public affairs of the time, not written out of the poet's personal experience. There have, of course, been important and moving 'political' poems written from within oppressed experience. Feminist poetry is certainly written from within the female experience but, by definition, it goes further than the personally political poetry which has cried out against, for example, war or slavery. Our work constitutes a challenge to the philosophical/religious constructs which underlie all human activity. Because women have not participated in deciding what is "natural", or what is "right", or what is "real", these controlling concepts have lacked an important reality and have oppressed us. Now we intend to expand, perhaps to burst, all these ideas, and each small poem, each act of consciousness raising, is part of this great collective work. The insights we bring in this way are at once deeply personal and of universal significance. Because this work gives us thoughts and feelings which we recognise in such an interior and personal way, we can not be bullied out of their universal implications. Genuine revolution ultimately depends on such steadfast internal knowledge.

The pressures which have created a large body of feminist poetry have also acted against carrying this new work outward to encompass a readership as broad as our vision must have if it is to be effective as a tool for change. Most of the poets published in this anthology have not been published before or have been published in pamphlets or magazines with a limited distribution. In small part, this is because Women's Liberation Movement publications have not had access to enough money to produce in great numbers or to distribute widely. Many women have deliberately chosen to keep their work from commercial publishers because they know they challenge male conceptions of reality and of worth and/ or because they do not wish to enhance the coffers or the reputations of establishment publishers.

After ten years, our own movement has developed various patterns which contradict the initial impetus of consciousness raising and which sometimes prevent giving poetry the recognition and attention which would make it most useful. Our conferences have grown to include thousands of women; few consciousness raising groups are springing up to encompass these new women; our political analyses have led to separate and often conflicting groupings whose statements are frequently constrained to the impersonal (not to mention the unsubtle). I feel Women's Liberation needs again to recognise the kind of insights feminist poets are labouring to reveal. To begin to write from within the female experience is still a new task — we are all unsure, not able to trust that our perceptions are not infiltrated by the pervading present patriarchal culture. Challenging every assumption, and then finding assumptions so old and deep we had not noticed them and challenging those too, has left us with little time for disseminating our work. This book is an attempt to remedy that. Nearly all our perceptions "are implanted through language — the all pervasive language of myth, conveyed overtly and subliminally through religion, 'great art', literature, the dogmas of professionalism, the media, grammar. Indeed, deception is embedded in the very texture of the words we use, and here is where our exorcism can begin."[1]

In selecting the work for this book I have tried to choose material which is clearly representative of feminist thinking and I have attempted to omit poetry which is obviously about those areas of feminism which overlap with other existing political ideologies (ie. socialism). In addition, I have selected work which seems to me to be really effective, moving, strongly put. All these choices involve a subjectivity which I hope will soon be accompanied by the production of other feminist anthologies displaying other sensibilities.[2]

Some women have objected to the element of individual recognition which is explicit in a book like this one, since our movement has been built upon a democratic approach to all our work and a resolve to abolish hierarchies. "One of the reasons the use of our names and the striving for greatness has been challenged is because of the association with male competitiveness. If A is great, then B can't be as great. There's only one slot at the top. The arts are somehow pyramidical. But for our very survival, women artists need to see ourselves as radiating outward from a center, doing many diverse things, but drawing constantly on each other's breakthroughs and discoveries."[3] Women are at last giving each other the respect and recognition so long denied by male systems and in this process, of course, we take public responsibility for our work. This identifying ourselves as the poets responsible for these words is done in the expectation of active readers, women who will search their minds (and other parts) for all the possible allusions which these poems could intend, women who will understand that this is dialogue, this is common labour.

Many poems in this anthology seek to describe the horror of our oppression. Women have been able to endure what is done to us without rising up to stop it, in part, by avoiding looking/seeing/acknowledging. We must have lots of these poems, enough to "deepen the anguish in every woman's heart until . . ." (Lucy Stone). These poems prevent us from forgetting the circumstances which make a Women's Liberation Movement necessary. Valerie Sinason's "That Girl" is one clear example of the power of such directed vision. Alison Fell's economical language becomes a branding iron, searing in the political import of what she tells us in "For Maria Burke". Others go on to state our intention to change these situations and Alison accomplishes this with sharp elegance in "Freedom Roads Song". Elsewhere, by completely redefining a common situation, change is already effected -- what would happen if women approached heterosexuality with the viewpoint Zoe Fairbairns produces in "The Thing You'll Like Best"?

Poems giving voice to our righteous rage like Diana Scott's "Poem for the Dark Goddess; on the full moon" clearly follow from these; as do Janet Dube's beautiful imperatives, steadfastly announcing that we will change the world. Statements of self-assertion (a very different business from self-fulfilment, the liberal con which holds up, and circles within, the status quo) and the struggle to make such assertion, to make oneself, ultimately, are another significant grouping of poems. Judith Kazantzis' "For J", for example, not only describes this necessity but displays through its tough language and inverted grammar some of the process of assertion itself. Stef Pixner shows us an interior landscape forced into being by this struggle in "THAT WORLD THROUGH THE WINDOW IS A BAREFACED LIE".

I have included several poems clearly written from within the movement, describing the particular work/life we have begun during the last ten years. Alison Fell might call it 'one foot on the mountain'; Thalia Doukas might say 'falling on nails'. These metaphors set up echoes for every feminist. More specifically, there are poems which deal with how we work together, our own emerging language, self-criticism, the new ways of living feminism has created for some of us. For example, Caroline Halliday's "November '77" is rooted in recent movement experience, giving other feminists the strength that comes from public acknowledgement, release from isolation. Here she considers several disparate incidents, ordering them in such a way that the reader leaps from one to the next making real and tangible an internal logic familiar to most women. Words, pictures, analyses, connections which often happen simultaneously in our heads can lose something important when separated. This poem, however, encourages the reader to feel the original dynamic, the simultaneity, while expressing it in the choppy grammar, the rush of images, the significant quotations. The many ideas/images she presents gather into a last line, "with a short haircut you cannot be grabbed by the hair". Yet this line also has the effect of a kind of radiating outward, forcing the birth of other images to do with experiences Caroline knows other women in the movement have had or might yet have. Ann Oosthuizen's poem about her writers' group, "Bulletins from the Front Line", invigorates, gives us a material sense of our courage as well as our anxieties. Paula Jennings speaks from within a lesbian feminist context, assuming an audience who shares that experience and is ready to smile/laugh at itself. Sheila Shulman's poem, "Hard Words", is a finely reasoned approach to the important new philosophical constructs which the positive assertion of lesbian feminism necessitates.

Within feminist circles there is a recognition that we must begin to change language so that it reflects our experience of the world. Traditionally, poetry is where one phrase or image stands for a collection of associations and thus reinforces connections or makes new ones. (The 'apple of her eye' must once have seemed an unusual way to put things. Metaphor becomes cliche, sticks in our consciousness.) Some poets in this anthology have begun to assume feminist associations for certain phrases and to use words to give us new assumptions. Some, like Barbara Zanditon in "In the British Museum" are describing their own relation to writing, confirming its importance to feminism. Deb Symonds speaks explicitly about the refashioning of language and literary concepts, "we will take language back to the body", while simultaneously using this nomenclature of the female body in ways not previously possible. Katherine Gabriella's long graphic description of a D&C makes poetry out of parts of our bodies which have, until recently, been romanticised, made clinical or made pornographic (essentially the same activity, erasing female reality). Mary Woodward assumes in her poem 'well, what do I want now that I'm nearly 32' that a feminist audience will have a new catalogue of meanings for the phrase "what i began to be" than we could have done before realising some of the particular strait-jackets male culture has imposed on us.

Sex, too, is described in the poetry in this anthology from inside female experience. Heterosexuality as a norm for women is not necessarily assumed. There are not a great many poems about sex included, in part because women have so long been seen only in sexual terms (either too pure for it or utterly insatiable) and now it seems appropriate to explore a great deal else.

Explorations/celebrations/reassessments of relationships between women make up another body of work represented in this book. The women described are not seen as love or hate objects; that is, they are not as men would have described us. Women are making new bonds, redefining old ones — exciting, difficult, necessary work. Sheila Shulman's 'Pome for Jackie' movingly states the case. (Of course, in some sense all the poems in this anthology could be said to be of this kind since they have been created out of what women are learning together in the women's movement.) In this area one will find material concerning mothers and daughters, one of the most difficult knots we have set ourselves to untangle/retie. Motherhood is considered both by women who are mothers and by women who are making other choices. Lesley Saunders, in "Hermana Madre", questions her situation as a mother while affirming deep loving connections with another mother, with mothers. Caroline Griffin's "The Child Bangs the Drum" is a poem full of penetrating observation as well as analytical challenge, exploring her relation to women who choose motherhood. Diana Scott's "Of Other People's Children", is another remarkable set of challenges and redefinitions. She shows us the delicate beauty of infants and places this delight alongside powerful attacks on the conventional view of these: 'I am in control of my own life/she said/meaning I own a child and can control her/to make up for the fact I am not free". Her depiction of the childless woman is no less disturbing (in this word's best sense), urging the reader toward reexamination.

Some of the poems in this volume have given us lines which I think will reverberate into our daily speech because they encapsulate something important, briefly and pithily. For example, the multiple implications in Chandra Masoliver's telling lines, 'we were not listening/to what we said' make sure that they will be said aloud and shared often. Janet Dube's couplet, 'Nothing we say's to be trusted/Nothing we say's a lie', is the sort of aphorism we need to and will remember.

I don't want to call humour a category, but I wish to point out that when writing about important feminist concerns some of the poets in this book have chosen to be very funny indeed — with snap and verve as in more than one of Paula Jennings' contributions, with wry subtlety as in Helen Ramsbottom's poem, "Beethoven", often with irony as in Michelene Wandor's work, or with fantasy as in Judith Kazantzis'.

The primary quality I have looked for in selecting these poems has been one of redefinition. The poems here are never resigned. Nothing is assumed to be inevitable or seen as "natural". Feminists have to be more conscious than anyone else. We must continuously see and say that what the world/men has declared invisible or invalid is real and important. Our descriptions, our analyses, our poems have force because they run counter to prevailing views and because we know they do. Fresh vision, contributions to the long task of renaming the world and our place in it — that's what I sought, and found.

In terms of relation to traditional academic standards of poetic craft, these poems vary widely. In part, this reflects the different kinds and degrees of involvement various women have had with these standards. My own internalisation of these is often difficult for me to find, let alone examine. So, I found that some of the poetry contributed to this book seemed inaccessible, too complex, at first — perhaps I mean it was too unlike other material. Other poems initially struck me as much too obvious. Rereading and rereading has changed at least some of my preconceptions. In concentraing on certain subjects, and in selecting these poems in the way that I have done, I recognise that other subjects have been left out, other definitions gone unchallenged. There is for example the omission of work by or about very young women as well as old women. There is the glaring omission of black poets. I have worked on what I am most familiar with in our movement in the expectation that other anthologies will publish in areas where I am inexperienced.

At least five women's writers' groups are represented in this book. The participants in these groups have made a large contribution to feminist poetry not only through their individual poems but through the increase in quantity as well as in intensity and purpose that this working together has created. A community of feminist writers is evolving. We have begun to help each other to write, to write for each other, to influence, to criticise, to destroy barriers and intimidations and old standards, and to construct working methods. Feminism has for many of us meant a loss of all our previous identifying securities. This is different from the existential alienation and dead-end isolation that many modern male poets have addressed. For women this stripping away has become an imperative to make new definitions, identities, connections. The work in this book comes out of the connections we are making, a collective sense of effort and of discovery. We intend to tell each other everything we can, every secret, because we know this intimate, difficult exchange makes a difference, is the process of change.[4] This anthology's poems are of passionate intention, provoking participation, because as feminists we are part of a dynamic which insists upon discussion and response. The community of women from whom these ideas have emanated will, I hope, respond, talk back, create new poems.

Lilian Mohin

footnotes

1 Mary Daly, *Gyn/Ecology: The Metaethics of Radical Feminism* (The Women's Press, London 1979).

2 This collection has been affected by the publicity Onlywomen Press could (or rather, could not) afford when soliciting material and by my personal acquaintance with a large number of poets.

3 Adrienne Rich, "poetry and women's culture", *The New Woman's Survival Sourcebook* (Alfred A. Knopf, New York, 1975) p.109.

4 Deena Metzger makes much the same point in her article, "In Her Image," *Heresies*, May, 1977.

There is no way I can adequately thank all the women who have contributed to the creation of this book. Still, I want particularly to thank the Women's Literature Collective, Astra, Caroline Gilfillan, Chandra Masoliver, Janet Dubé, Judy Barrington, Judith Kazantzis, Sally Berry, and Sheila Shulman, because, over a period of six years, we worked together on many of the ideas that have come to fruition here. With and through Judy Barrington I learned to keep changing, keep writing; this book is part of that. Jacky Bishop's insight and dedication to Onlywomen Press have been especially valuable. Brenda Whisker has given heroic amounts of energy, time, and clear feminist thinking to the creation and nurturing of Onlywomen Press. Anna Wilson has given me the indispensable support of true friendship throughout the making of this anthology, as well as the benefit of her searching criticism and a lot of plain hard work. There are so many others — all the women who have given inspiration, encouragement, information, ideas, criticism, and dreams to me and to the other poets in this book, the women who are the women's liberation movement.

ALISON FELL

Born Scottish borders 1944, spent five years at Edinburgh Art College. Son born 1967. Met women's movement in Leeds 1970. Co-founded Women's Street Theatre group in London 1970. Worked on underground newspaper 'INK', then Islington Gutter Press, Red Rag, and since 1975, Spare Rib. Poems and stories and drawings published in Spare Rib, Cutlasses and Earrings, *and* Licking the Bed Clean. *Currently in a women writers collective.*

Love Song — the beginning of the end of the affair

I lie across your bed, love
Three cats and your children enfold me.
These necklaces I would never wear —
for I was a wild boy-girl —
at last
you, love
have twined them all around me.

Hungers move my heart now
but where will we touch, which
layers meet, my lovely flyer,
bird of air? You race, you soar,
raise winds, string perfect cloudstreams
in your wake.

But I am the woman with
one foot on the mountain,
my tread turns earth
and my stumblings are moving me beyond you.

Pinned to my mirror for you
I leave my blonde hair,
my pout, and other scraps,
refractions:
was that not all you wanted?

Rage I have now,
squalls of delight;
grief bursts hot and salt
on my cheek.
It's so lonely here
I wanted a companion.
But to ask you
is to see only your flinch,
and then a sudden shadow
in the corner of my eye
a mote in the sky
darting.

Women in the Cold War

Outside, time and famous dates passed —
Korea Suez Cuba Algeria all cannoned by
casually as a slap on the back.
In the butcher's and the grocer's,
not a word of them. No, only talk of
the sun, snow, seasons;
stillbirths, new banns posted;
the harvest, the Gala,
the Foot and Mouth which closed farm roads,
the Compensation.
As for violence, we had our own —
a thousand cattle burned in pits
a labourer, demented, raped a child
fine swimmers drowned in the loch's depths.
And most Saturdays some girl's wedding
brought the women clattering
down the High Street — they'd bang
on doors along the way and put up the cry,
then hang back respectfully and squint
at the hired cars, the ceremonial clothes.
My mother, her mother's mother

were brides like these,
country brides teetering up
the gravel-chipped path to the Kirk,
shielding their new shoes from scrapes.
By the sandstone wall, photos were posed,
against a bleak swell of lowland hills;
the photos show puckered faces
and a wind which sweeps the stiff bouquets.
The dances came and went, and fashions;
my girlfriends and I — in tight skirts
(or tiered), beads which popped
and hooped net petticoats —
crushed into cars and choked
on our own close scent, and smoke, and compliments.
But soon they sobered and they planned —
knitted cardigans all summer, by January
scanned the catalogues for cottons,
drab (for work), dressy (for holidays).
I saw them smooth
and full-blown dreaming of marriage
when I was still pockmarked with envy
and a thousand wants. I became crazy:
'I'll be an artist' I said
and bristled for the skirmish; quite slowly
their eyes scaled and their good sense
bunched against me.
'That's no' for the likes o' us'.
Elizabeth, Elaine, Rhoda of the long legs,
all matrons, mothering, hurrying
their men to work at 7am.
Now, hunched round prams,
what landmarks of content do they stake out
as the village circles?
As tractors streak the fields with lime
and all the old women, hushed,
move to the funeral to see the flowers.

Girl's gifts

The soft whorls of my fingertips
against snapdragons:
I am making a flower basket for my grandmother.
A rose petal folds back, squares, curls under

One, two, many rose petals curl back
between my fingers
I search for the core which hides.
My grandmother is gentle today,
old. Bees hum over her.
Today she sits reading, not gardening,
not scolding.
The blossom on its branch holds juice which
a touch spills
I glance across the grass,
a shadow in the window is my mother
cooking, watching.
I am making a tiny secret basket for my grandmother.
My mouth waters
I would lick the green leaf, taste the bronze
and yellow silk of my snapdragon,
I mould petals, weave stems, with love
my little finger inches in the folds:
it is done, red and gold.
I will carry it cupped like a jewel or a robin's egg
It will lie, perfect, in her wrinkled palm
I will cross the grass and give it.

Freedom Roads Song

Spirit springs a bit now,
escape route set up, sun's
coming on again,
time for me to go, right?
like men in songs do.

First pain pinches, off they
flip, freewheeling, freeloading,
regular roadrunners.
Somebody told them the future
belonged to them, and anyway
women always wait, right?
women in songs do.

Lover doesn't need me, got a wife
to brood on
Wife doesn't need him, got another

to dote on.
Lover wants to gag me,
I talk too much, heavy stuff,
it nags at him.
Makes me feel like a ghoul
time for me to go, right?

Past snaps at my heels
its losses, contortions
This gymnast needs to spring now,
like men in songs do.
Who ever told me the future
belonged to me,
that kiss
and that promise?

Old Dreadful

I can't stop it.
The night drags down on
me and
the beast is out,
scraggy, cawing
for man-flesh or
someone-skin.
What an endeavour,
living with this nag under
the rafters.
(Normally it nests quietly
enough, sullen
in the straw and shade,
I feed it chocolate slyly)
Now it booms round the
room and plops down,
romps sideways, an old flirt
in thin feathers,
tucks its head under the
arms of strangers, points
a claw, wheedling,
nudges, thrusts up
its red mouth wide.

Atlanta Streets

The timidest man owns streets
with his eyes — headlights sweeping
breasts, lips, thighs —
they dip only for a bigger bruiser.

Our lowered eyelids hide murder.

Outside a drugstore in Atlanta
one thug tried it on, for him
we waited, four of us fringing
the sidewalk, gangsters in the
shadows. One flung a chocolate malted
in his face, he lunged
kicked her down while we paused
(everyone hesitates who fears the murder
in her) but only for the time the bright
sour pink of a police car beacon
takes to spin once,
and then these sisters beat and clawed him
down and when he tried to run
I caught his coat-tails
and he spun back, roaring,
in an arc
into their fists again
and still I stalled there —
until his buddy came to even up
the odds, then I was ready, but then
there was glass shattering
and the ruby razor neck of a
Coke bottle crooked up, glistening
and obscene,
and wise blacks hanging back
and white folks coming close — to
gawp? defend? who? us? him?
the staggering ravaged guy?
And now it was time to run, vault,
dodge trash, make
scant wind in the
still city dark, to the
car-park, rev through the underpass
shudder out to the
Freeway's tungsten howl

FOR MARIA BURKE (who knocked at the door while I was writing
about the alienation of life in the cities under capitalism.)

Maria, in search of hospitality:
I opened the door a crack
she stood there in the dark
dribbling a bit.
'We're in need of somewhere to stay'
She was alone. It was winter.
She wore plimsolls, her bare legs
were hairless.
'I used to know some man who lived here.
It's a squat, isn't it.'
'No, not a squat,' I snapped,
'And who was the man?'

The powerful deeply suspect
the powerless
of manipulations and lying.

'You should come in from the cold.'
Maria's eyes were fixed,
glassy on largactyl.
I phoned some hostels;
she knew them all and
loathed them, said she'd crouch
by frozen trees in the park
rather than go there.
'I went to a house I used to
live in, it was all pulled down'.

Clocks and towers loom over her
Homes shudder and tumble around her.

Her hands shook eating soup.
She accepted tea.
'It's the drug makes me shake'.
She'd hitched from a mental home
in Manchester, heading for another
in Southall, which didn't want her.
'I've a letter from the consultant.
Will you phone for me, tell him
I'm coming in?'

It was dated last June,
it said merely 'Dear Maria,
it was pleasant to see you
at the hospital today. What
I explained to you is that the drug
is a chemical which acts
on the brain and is necessary
to stabilise the thought processes.'

'It's my only home' said
the orphan angrily, 'I know
they don't want me
but I'm going in. I was there . . .
I lived there . . . three years.'
I showed her the spare room
she thanked me several times
stripped to her bra while
I was still there.
Only those with homes are entitled
to modesty, the consultant
is modest, his wife is modest
her body belongs to him only;
Maria's belongs to anyone:
the mouth to nurses who feed it
the head to doctors who shock it
the nipple to drivers on the open road
who pluck it
the smooth skin to the casual helper.

The consultant, who has all he needs,
considers her promiscuous, recoils
from the glare of her love that
stares from her eyes, seeking.
He reaches for a prescription pad;
this winter, he decides,
Maria must stand on
her own two plimsolls.

Maria gathering up
selves scattered like
grit on the roadside
doodles darkness
and a cottage with lit windows,
gropes and pines for her
three-minute-a-fortnight
father.

ANGELA HAMBLIN

is a feminist writer. Her work has appeared in Women's Liberation Review, Spare Rib, *and* Conditions of Illusion: Papers from the Women's Movement.

She has also edited and published The Other Side of Adoption, *a book dealing with the life-long but often hidden suffering of many unmarried mothers who were forced to give up their babies for adoption.*

To Astra

like a breath of fresh air
your poems enter my life
making me stop
momentarily
to consider your struggles
                with the world
                with feminism
                with your self

i read them
                with affection
                with respect
but above all
                with recognition
                of your search
                for authenticity.

we met
last week
in a coffee bar
almost like lovers
and stole
an hour
from our busy lives
           to plan
                 plot
                 analyse
                 discuss
                 and understand

i was high all day.

we tread our
separate paths
you and i
and that feels
right somehow
but we travel
the same road

what are we?
           friends
           colleagues
           crusaders?
           (to use Kate's word)
i don't know
i just know that
           what i recognise
           in you — is
           what i see in myself

Recognition —
           i guess that's
           what it's all
           about
i really know
           you
           woman-friend
and i like what
           i know.

ANNA WILSON

*Born September 1954 in the Home Counties. A civil servant. Became a lesbian
early, in confusion and disgust and rebellion. Feminism, an identity, and liking
women are later, precarious, precious additions. Our version of reality is always
under siege and my grasp of meaning tenuous, but I aspire to understand/
describe/change the world (it shall have me in it, this time). And to be other than
a civil servant.*

we stand close
for many months
you look over my shoulder
i get to know
your neck   well

yesterday
your postcard said
'stagnation'

i do not feel   secure but

i have nothing to lose so

medusa   open your raincoat

◫ In doorways
swathed bodies
embrace cheeks
touch
cumberous winter arms
entwine

women touching
their slow flapping dance
a rite of friendship

I see beneath each cold embrace
a caress
lusting for birth

they move off down the street
hands as they pass
ruffling my hair

◫ she and I went on holiday together
once. She wore blue and said
she was enjoying herself even
that she was enjoying me
so when she said let's
go on holiday I thought
wow she's enjoying me
again still think of that
and I said Great. Where shall
we go?

She said I really
NEED to eat SQUID you
see I am insufficiently replete and
I need to rest. With you, dear,
of course. Well I said
I know a place in New
York sells the best . . .

Oh no she said
When I said squid I meant
Me? I said
No she said Squid.
And no distractions.

So she went off carrying
a lot of toothpicks
and saying see you later
and that was last
spring and actually about
two months ago I received
a postcard, it said
I don't want to
disappoint you (it said)
because I am really fond
of you (really you know it
said that, so she must have
enjoyed the first holiday)
but have not yet
experienced
satiety. Yours

but I have been thinking of
how she used to read National
Geographical Magazines with such
interest and how her grasp
of metaphor was so vivid and
so physical
and suddenly my mind is full
of long-armed Cretan ladies

Non-Violence or The Feminist Way of Death

warrior queen   strategist
beating the enemy
at their own game
the light in her eyes hiding
the scrunch of bone

but that's all mystification
modern warfare's a different high
you can do anything
from a distance
the clean whine of a bullet
shatters glass with abstract purity
the moment of fragmentation
just perfect

in judo class i learn
to throw   women
i learn how strong men are
i learn my limitations
more useless knowledge

ANN OOSTHUIZEN

is a feminist who lives in London. She has written poems and stories about events in her own life in an attempt to analyse experience rather than just to endure it. She has been married, widowed, a student, a lecturer, a teacher, a youth worker, a theatre director, a mother, a lover, a daughter, a friend, a grandmother. She is half way through her life and wants a lot more from it.

My Holiday

To a lunch party in Ibitha
The man from the BBC
Brings three cameras and a boyfriend.
He takes a movie of this group
Of English abroad, sitting
Negligently on a roof-top.
All the island is spread around us
As he jumps about.
It's got a lovely zoom, he says
In St Lucia Bay I could zoom in
On black dongs :zoom, zoom.
They giggle.
But it hasn't been the same, he says, since
I took a picture of me mum (the camera, he means).

Peter holds a gin and tonic and finds him
Enormously funny.
Elaine poses on his lap
Polly golly doodle all the dong, she warbles
But he's off again with another camera
Clicking at a woman with an armful
Of two little girls. Lovely, he says
Portrait of a mother as a young mother.
Forever Mother, I think, until you're Mum
And break the camera.

Having zipped up his zoom he starts
A long story about someone called Chris
Who phoned at four in the morning
Asking to share their bed, when he
Our hero, had to be on location at six-thirty.
And Linda, that liberated woman
Who dared request a lift
Let her pay for a taxi, why should he help
When her car's broken down and she needs a ride
She's liberated and must take the consequences.

Frankly, I'd rather.
As we climb into cars, he fishes a large piece
Of green slime out of the farmer's pond,
Look, he cries, a mermaid's sanitary towel!
Peter giggles like a schoolboy at his wit
Isn't he quick, he nudges his wife
Did you hear what he said, just like that?
A mermaid's sanitary towel
Yes, dear, she replies.

    ⌗ I do not remember you with pleasure,
Sometimes when I sit, for example
Next to a river shaded by tall trees
And hear the music of the water
As it shapes itself over the folded rocks,
I am reminded that we were once
Together by such a river
And that you held me there in your arms.
Then it is as if a deep shadow
Closes thick and dark over my mouth and nose.
My heart beats fast, in terror.
Is this what I felt then?

If we meet again in that other world
Two shades, as Milton said,
Insubstantial and without sex,
I will not run to you.
There is no part of me that consents
To being one with you.
You owned me once and strutted over
The territory that was me,
Marking it with your mark, fencing it well,
Pulling out weeds that grew there.
You planted your seed in me,
You have fulfilled your god's command.
And I?
Barren is not sparse enough to describe
The fear and fright that grew in me
Only a tiny speck of mine remained.
You worked on that
And so did I; my guilt equal to your zeal,
But there was that in me which said;
I am not all yours.

Now you are dead.
I mourn for you.
I wish that you had known happiness
That you had found a gentle, wholesome love.
It was not so. My guilt made me spiky,
My barrenness grew sharp stones under your feet
You did not find peace in your small-holding.

This plot of land is for sale no longer.
If we meet again, you will say:
What a rocky landscape, give me richer earth.
That is how I want it to be.
This land is mine.

Bulletins from the front line

Regimental HQ, Ali's room;
Three windows, two desks, one bed
Papers everywhere.
Five women meet; a council of war
Our strategy still unspoken.
We are not in uniform, there are no medals,
We read the latest bulletins from the front line
Carefully we study the terrain together.

Outside this blue room where dreams
Caress the tall green plants
Cars move on highways;
"Hey Baby", another woman raped.

We will asault all.
Tina, menacing at a window
Exquisite markswoman aims,
Her sniper's bullet finds unerring home.
Ali tunnels underground
Mining each foundation with precision
The city crumbles in surprise.
While Stef, laughing, flies overhead
Drops bombs without looking
Blows the world to smithereens.
What power, Sisters!
Michele's a pacifist, she says,
She disregards the war
Stands on the highest building
Look at me!
Her ear-rings challenge sun and moon,
Here it is, the war
In me, start here.

Five women plan in the smoke blue room;
Silence brings a pause for fear
Am I good enough? each one asks
Hesitating

The cold draught has caught
An old war-wound in me.
I smile, my deaths-head smile
My skull cracks open.
I rattle goodbye across the railings.
As I pass through the park
There is no cover.
Shell-shocked, I limp home my old bones aching.

ASPEN JOYCECHILD WOMUN

Aspen (populus tremula) is a tree with trembling leaves and interesting autumn colouring. She has a light, porous, but surprisingly tough wood, which burns slowly. She is quite unsafe near buildings as she can cause soil shrinkage which disturbs the foundations. The female variety is extremely unpoplar with nurserymen as her hairy catkins blow everywhere and are extremely difficult to eradicate. Always rich in insect life, aspen is a thirsty tree preferring swamps, river gravels, and mountain screes. She began as a sucker in Derby and is at present growing in Fife.

I am being born a woman human being
I have breasts and a soft body
I am made of soil and water and I look like a tree
I have quite a few scars, but I am growing more beautiful everyday
not more perfect, just more me.
I have lost quite a bit of blood at the hands of jagged men cultivating me for
commercial interest
I have removed myself from their cultivated plots
where every tree must strive to look the same
and be quiet and obedient
and bear fruit (of the right kind) at their bidding
I have picked up my roots and wriggled my toes and stepped out gingerly into
the world

I have not always had enough moisture to blossom forth
I may move again
Someone said (I dont know who) "women are the best trees that grow"
Outside the forestry commission we roam the hills
and sniff life.

⊠   i cry out
all you hear is a moan on the wind
i lay forth my truths
you hear a squeak in the corner
i scuttle along and metamorphose
you see bizarre shapes with no meaning
i insist you pay attention
you say my bullshitting is done very well

i beat you about with my anger
you laugh at my attempts to hurt you
i cover you sloppily in love
you walk away looking out of the corner of your eye
i weep in frustration
you catch my tears and sell them to the tourists
i whisper in despair
you pour sympathy on my fallen crest

i collapse in a heap on the floor
you cart me off to your nearest bin
i create the most amazing art
you pity my disturbed mind
i sing the most lovely woman-songs
you moralise over my bent sexuality
i make the most wonderful sense
you say you do not understand . . .

when did you stop listening to me?
do i have to use words that don't hurt your ears so much?

⊠   I have watched you
running along careless
laughing, dancing
watching me.

Your curious observations in my direction
unnerve me . . .
What are you doing?

i watch you unawares
small breasts pushing childhood away
you on the verge:
eleven years old
smooth brown arms, hands reach to touch
body moves close, black hair on my arm
what are you doing?

I only want to look at you
and touch you, kiss your mouth
hold your body in magic embraces
like a lover
speak gently
laugh loudly
read, play, sing, dance
call your name in the night
watch you sleeping in my arms . . .

your brown eyes are falling all over my face
are you in love with me?
I panic.

I'm struggling with the contradictions:
your paranoid parents have laid cornflakes between us
I flush, toilet fashion, under their stare.
Our elastic interaction which no one must see
waxes and wanes, your body close to mine
pulls us nearer, stretches
(i can't bear it) stretches . . .
. . . and snaps.

for lyser

gravely i burn the dancing candle
and taste the flames   let me
drink your wet smooth body
my slow, lazy, discovering love
emerges
the waves uncurl

i long for your breast
cheek on cheek, lips feel
lips, our skin, your hair my hair
our legs entwine enfold
can you feel the surge, the
swarm, this mad joy swallow us whole
fall sinking through
we flow needing
pressing
skin on skin, breast on breast
careful, gentle fingers stroke
me inside me
nursing her womb tongues entwine
belly rises, we go under
immerse, emerge
fold your chin on my neck
hands in my hair
your seaweed excitement
dripping puddles on my legs
i rise carefully   let me
breathe your ocean   flow
into me into you   feel
the soft colourful sea bed   let me
breathe your ocean   rise
on your waves   feel
the swell   let me
breathe your ocean   taste
your flood.

for my "apolitical" sisters

i am so *hostile* you say
when i struggle to break my chains

i am so *extreme* you say
when i say all women are oppressed

i am *unrealistic* and *impractical*, even *mad* you say
when i say we must consciously refuse to take care of men

i have become so *political* you say . . .
sister, i've got news for you:
your "inactivity" is also a political statement . . .

listen:
oppression is not a choice
or just the misfortune of the socially deprived
no woman has escaped
sexism falls like quiet rain
constantly, softly seeping in
until we all become saturated
and it gently, ever so gently
so we hardly notice
does us terrible violence,
the ice forms, moulding us into
a shape uncannily uniform, uncannily
suitable for men.
oppression is not a choice, to fight it IS
we must stir the springs of liquid fire
in every woman, every child,
flames to burn the last wail of male arrogance
from our minds and hearts and bodies.

until then
when you nurture his ego, offer your body,
wash his socks, raise his children,
you are being a political activist too.

ASTRA

I've been an amerikan ex-patriate since early 1962 but didn't enter the Women's Liberation Movement till mid-1971; since then my life style and my politics have been irrevocably altered. In 1972 I joined the women's literature collective where I began taking myself seriously as a poet. That group developed into a feminist writers' group which produced 4 anthologies of our prose & poetry. Currently I'm working on a collection of poems about my mother.

Some of the other areas I write my poems around include amerika, celibacy, divorce, family life, friendship, growing older, holidays, living alone, marriage, motherhood, my aunt, my cats, my childhood, my dad, my garden, my ex-husband, my radical feminist politics, my sons, separatism, the women's movement, writing (& not writing).

gift giving

you give me gifts
so i'll love you
i'll love you as long as
you give me gifts you think

the more you need me
my love
the more you give me
the more you give me
the less i need you

the less i give you
the more you want me
the more you want me
the less you'll ever let down your defenses

so if i give you a present
                              will you let me be?

more recollections

each early spring or late winter
pussy willows crocuses snow drops pink skies
commandeer her back to me

we never strolled together
except a few times in pennsylvania
when she came to visit me at summer camp
though i'd wanted not walks
but sitting with her talking with her being with her:
our bodies making contact

she never ceased to love my dad
though god knows she had cause enough
yet she never spoke against him
though he was the one who made her gaiety recede
and melancholy predominate:
he hardly missed a moment
to denigrate her   and all women
and when i displeased him he'd say
just like your mother   just like a woman

i didn't like him much —
mostly i wished he'd just go away

sometimes she walked naked around our apartment
wearing only shoes
(after he'd left us)
much to my embarrassment
especially if i returned home with a girlfriend
but she ended this before i was an adolescent

without ever saying why
but then we'd never discussed it at all —
her doing it and my hating it

she talked endlessly of her office life —
the politics and personalities —
and probably puffed up her own importance in the typing pool
but i followed each day's recital with avid interest
and endorsed her aspersions on everyone

as to my own life those teenage days ago —
did i talk much about it   to her   to anyone —
friends   school   teachers
and boys?
my keenest memories are of her nagging me to go out with boys
though afterwards she ridiculed their imperfections
and i concurred: i always did —
i preferred being with girls anyway

all the while she talked more and more
of our being like sisters (was that to stop me leaving home?)
with me liking the notion less and less
and squirming inside myself:
she never knew

nor could she have imagined how much i loved her
four decades past

direction: to my mother

i want not to walk in her footsteps
her erratic troubled tracks
laid down early in this century
on the lower east side of manhattan —
the immigrants' new world ghetto
of overpeopled stalls shops schools
and steaming apartment cells
facing bricked walls and treeless yards —
everything she loathed
till she died

i want not to hear her family directing her in yiddish
to be
    serious
    studious
    soft spoken
    scrubbed
    smiling
    and married soon
    to a doctor   please god

she wasn't   any of these

nor was i: we had that in common
yet even she wanted a doctor son in law
after all

sometimes i feel i am her
especially when anger with my kids overwhelms me
and i sense my features following hers
despite my best intentions

did she suspect how like her mother she was?

elsewhere

you can't go home again someone said
once
or twice
now i believe it

i devote so much energy to
avoiding people who say
they're dying
            to see me
somehow they survive
while i die
            of boredom
                    making excuses
                            to avoid them

i'll not go home again
because my home
            is elsewhere

opiate

how well each happylittlefamily
makes possible benevolent violence
both physical and verbal
how well the well intentioned autocracy
that is family
instills lifelong submission
how tightly this claustrophobic unit
closes up to anyone
not in its clan
how easily this insitution
overrides its members
in the guise of good humoured concern
how beautifully it turns out humans
who slot quickly into their roles
of spouse/worker/consumer/producer
and who rarely challenge the hierarchies in
the family/school/corporation/government
(when anyone dares too much
that fool is bought up
or shot down)

even revolution preserves the
sacredfamily
knowing how indispensible its services!
each new regime deliberately fosters
repression of the
sexuality of kids and women
and nothing really changes
at all:
        spouse/worker/consumer/producer
        all remain oppressed
because the illusion of the
happylittlefamily
is the
opiate
we dare not kick

coming out celibate

like men
so many women cannot imagine
friendship creativity existence
without sexuality
or what passes for sexuality
so that when i say
i am celibate
smiles of embarrassment appear
and the subject is quickly changed

i am awarded
pity or contempt or simply bewilderment
that i should not do
sexual things with and to
another person
preferably of the other gender
but anyway with someone for god's sake
since it's
"abnormal/unnatural/undesirable/and especially immature"
not to be dependent on someone
some of the time
for sexual satisfaction

i'm celibate from lack of opportunity surely:
it couldn't be my very own
consciously taken decision
could it?
because sleeping alone
even more than living alone
is seen as self denial
isn't it
especially if i like it that way:
i just need to meet the right person   don't i?

we must all be seen in
couples
families even "broken" families
collectives
some sort of relationship
all our lives
whether we like it or not
anything but as individuals   being glad in our one-ness

celibacy is more about autonomy than specific sexuality
celibacy is about choosing one's own
                              life style
                              friendships
                              ways of
                                          working doing being
and putting them all together
at different times

imagine an epidemic of autonomous individuals
and you're on your way to
realising a few feminist fantasies

BARBARA A. ZANDITON

Born 27 May 1944 in Boston, Massachusetts during a thunderstorm, the second of three daughters. Began writing poetry at 15 — dreadful stuff about death. Scared the life out of my mother who found it but had the grace to keep her mouth shut until many years later. I thought for a long time, because there was no one to tell me otherwise, that to be a "real" writer I had to learn to write like a man. Never got the knack of it and learned instead to trust my own, female, voice. Married an Englishman in 1974 and seem to have settled in London. If life were perfect, I would live by the sea and dream.

In the British Museum

Usually,
I go unheeding through this corridor
lined with false gods from someone else's country.
But today I do not get away with it.

Look, I tell them,
I was only passing through . . .
They demand attention.

This is not a department store
where one considers wares without commitment.
Here we are already committed —
by virtue of having been born.
History is an endless procession —
of women opening their legs and giving birth.

I am a woman. I bear witness to generations.
And to those generations where false gods played their part.
I do not think that I could worship stone idols
or love to see the blood spurt thick from some dumb beast.
But these things happened
and a woman wept and trembled
and in her safely slept a seed
which bore a seed
which bore a seed . . .

So I sit down
and I consider you a while
and I accept my obligations
and give you this.

THE BIG TEASE LADY PLAYING GAMES WITH DEATH

for Anne Sexton

There you are you sexy temptress witch
There you are you bitch
    teasing at me
    mocking at me
    from the back cover of your book

Oh you delectable lady
Six foot under
Where have you gone
Leaving your words

Those damnable words
    that poke at me
    prick at me
    force me to respond

Where have you gone so carelessly?

Was it terrible
Did you fear
Or feel regret
At that last moment — too late
Just as you lost control
Just as you lost it all

Oh beautiful lady
        I have loved too late
        for flesh and blood love of you
        would you have mocked me then
        as you do mock me now

Your image an infinitesimally thin kiss
On the shiny back cover of a book

For Rebekah After Two Years . . .

        when I only want to say
        something tender
        about your face
        and the fine new lines etched — so eloquent — upon it
        when I only want to say
        that the loving bond is still so strong
        I can think of no words, my sister

for my sister

        Last night
        I was reading your old letters
        and I thought
        that if someone read them in a hundred years
        they would think we were lovers.
        Would they be wrong?

Suffolk Sketches

I There is
   the company of other women
   I love
   in talk bright kitchens
   warm sunlight
   steaming
   into mugs of tea
   held by hands
   made capable with caring.

   Later
   we walk
   sunlit along the river
   talking against the wind
   the curlews cry sweet and clear.

II 2 heads
   mother and daughter
   sharing common
   memories and
   a smile

III You sketch
   quick light movements
   I tremble over words.

⊠ This year
I am wearing the more fully-fashioned
bosom.

My husband says
it's due to his attentions.

I say
I'm over thirty.
Time to spread out.
Get comfortable.

WISHING TO CUT THROUGH TO BONE — I

WISHING to cut through to bone
Cut off by daylight domesticities
Compelled by domesticities and gossip
The deep rooted trivia of lives . . .
I am moved by surfaces:
Light dancing on water
Light and shadow, playing on the crystal hard surfaces of water.

I AM AFRAID of going under.
Fearful of grit
Or salt
Or the brittle chlorinated pools of country clubs
Where oiled and basting, wet and sweating
We drink from lipsticked lips through straws inserted into six
inches of crushed ice packed into Sweetheart paper cups.

PLUNGING
Plunging, I emerge to surfaces.
I will begin again.

LOCKED in trivia
My life revolves on surfaces like a dancer on ice
The sharp edges of the skates shishing into ice
Like a glass cutter's wheel marking a line to tap along
Breaking the fine hard glass
The careful surface of the glass

I WILL BEGIN AGAIN
As often as necessary
I will begin again
to gain the risk of dancing on the polished floor . . .

WISHING TO CUT THROUGH TO BONE — II

Hard and cruel
Hard and cruel
NOW I am cutting into you
Cutting with my knife

No dull blade for butter this
but a sharp scalpel
Sharp enough for cutting through the tough carcus
hanging in the butcher's shop

The knife rests in my hand
handle against palm
forefinger pressed along the top

Head down
Head down
Now I am cutting into you
I am the Great Surgeon
dissecting the heart of darkness

Gently I run my knife across your belly
Then with a sudden force
plunge the blade deep into your skin
through fat through muscle down to bone

The Great Surgeon
disembowels
descends into the stinking flesh
cuts away to bone
and finds the heart
the wet heart
palpitating slick red organ
glistening
bloody
mocking.

CAROLINE GILFILLAN

I grew up in a seaside town in Sussex.

My first passion was for horses, but at 18 I left home and worked as an au-pair girl in Paris, an experience which left me with very little self-confidence and a distrust of men. I then hung around the fringes of the Far Left, until their exploitative treatment of women finally got to me. Then, five years ago, I came across the Women's Movement and felt, for the first time, that I had 'come home'. All my time and energy is now directed towards women. At present, I am working as a driver in Australia, but looking forward to returning to the vitality of London. I am now trying to write science fiction and short stories.

blood that we are taught to hate
dirty menstrual blood staining clothes
smelling unfresh and unclean
recalling butchers' shops and corpses
childbirth reproduction and death
teenage years of hiding sanitary towels
stuffing them in incinerators
choking on the ritual stink of grey smoke
my mother beckoning quietly   saying

45

i flushed the toilet again
you shouldn't leave that there
with men in the house   and
she was referring to the brilliant
red blood clot that remained and
flowered with transparent petals
into the water
                    ten years later
i am in a kitchen
a cat and mouse for company
and the moon has stroked
the pool of my stomach
ruffled the tepid waters
with untying of the knot
falling out of blood
in silky red strands
trailing soft like hair
on a pillow indented
with the smell of loving

in between typing i sit
and the muscles tucked
in the pelvis are tugged
and my spirit or what
may be called the root
is gathered and rolled

blood tasting sweet
smelling fresh of
vagina skin and uterus

this is the blood
we are taught to hate

you have put out my one eye
my sexual eye
with your light wet body
because I have fallen in love with you

are you nervous you say
no I reply
my body giving the truth
my mouth the lie
I have no practice in love
I shake like a creature learning to walk
after years of idleness
you stir into life
the confusion and ignorance
this stirring is painful
and I wonder if you'll stay around
through all the shaking and clumsiness
this doubt makes other doubts
harder to control

despite all this I'm over the moon
when we touch
two thin wires cross
I want to give you everything
and more   and more

lesbian play on t.v.

there has been a play on t.v.
a voyeuristic lesbian tale
the leading woman has a hard unvarnished
face   flat tits   dirty hands
her fate is some cruel joke   dreamt up
in script rooms over beer-guts and smoke
stale coffee   and earnest liberalism

take a deep breath   for she is a
potsmoking christian artist lavatorycleaner
workingclass raped byherfatherattheageof11
bisexual motorbykeriding   lesbian
everything goes wrong for her all all all all
the wrong decisions   she has lost her
virginity her child lost her youth her freshness
her best (prostitute) friend her debby lover
her paintings her home even her oinkish sugar daddy

the love-making scenes are the funniest/sickest
the leading actress allbutch gets into bed
with her trousers on (no frank love scenes please)
when they kiss it is all violence on her part
hard mouth and smouldering glances

II

there's been some sort of mistake
the lesbian I know is
unsupported mother   printer
factory worker   barmaid   student
musician   van driver   waitress
mother   daughter   child   grandmother
fat thin spotty smooth beautiful
vain hairy timid fucked-up
happy angry   she is bullied
or pampered   loved or unloved
she touches other women sexually
sometimes in shame   mostly in joy
she dreams   she writes this poem

47

✠ my mother looks very well
her neat grey hair fashioned like a hat
reminding me of a horse's hoof
with its folded contours
her cardigan is self-knitted
bright daisy-eye yellow
i greeted her with a pot of flowers
                 with affection

    she is alarmed at my going to australia
i brought some variety
and i am sorry to go
or rather not to know
               her better
without sentimentality
    i wish to approach her
but many things hold me back
    cowardice   tact   fear

nonetheless i love to see her
a very separate person
quizzical   solitary   woman
still my protectress
    first flesh on mine

✠ to be honest   your new friendship
left me unsure   our contact being so new
yet i detected some change   days before
a bite in the air   prickle of the scalp
whistle of the parting of the air   cleft by
some event   somewhere else   and this incision
reached me   knocked the breath from me
collapsed the sails   flying gold and high
quite impractical   before you said a word

all evening i felt angry   and windblown
i fumed and fidgeted   at the complications i make
swallowed a great many feelings   until they were coiled
at the base of my spine   dark and insistent
to conclude   we watched television
i observed the marked orange cheeks of janis ian
rolled up my shirt sleeves   while quietly
your curved fingers rested   on my forearm

⊠   i am expecting a revival
                              and i have had
        a touch of solitude like   lemon juice on the tongue
    birdsong from the blue
                              a little cut to the pink quick
            stinging grass blade touch

            and to my great surprise
                                  i am unscarred

    there is an emptiness soon to be dilated
        by writing   by pleasure   by the unexpected
    it is strange
                        how we rediscover   ourselves
    the spirit or centre   muscle behind the movement
        marrow in the bone
                                quite suddenly
    a door blown open   a derelict shed
                                a chair someone has just vacated

    and as the emptiness speaks
                                i listen

CAROLINE GRIFFIN

I was born 31 August 1950 and have three sisters.

I came to know women in the Women's Movement two years ago while learning African drumming. It is through sharing music and writing with women who are working at what being a feminist means that I have felt these activities to be powerful and political.

I am still teaching English at a London boy's comprehensive.

Being a lesbian and a feminist involves me in a struggle to make a world women might choose to live in — writing can suggest these worlds.

 The child bangs the drum.
He is your sister's child and
A rehearsal for your child.

In stuffy pubs, cold streets and wrinkled sheets
I've pressed this thought-child to me.
I've seen it born and you
Changed and secretive, consumed
With love perhaps or
Some justification for your diminished self.

A child can be no better one I suppose
To eat the discontent you live in
And grow sturdy. (Never fat.
Your sister's child eats fruit, not sweets.)

It makes me cry
To be so lacking all that world
Of tired mother-hood, penances
Of wakeful nights and always
To feed, to clean, to touch —
A vision clearer, old, will mark your effort.

A call so clearly just must be ignored.
I know if I don't eat I'll starve
And then my cry is bread.
What are you hungry for?
The easy vision?
The inevitable result?

I have no answer to that pure cry,
You're not my mother. But
I want my cries to be unreasonable,
Demanding cries. Older
How to answer them is difficult,
But no less urgent.

CHANGES OF TIME AND PLACE

Tomorrow is hungry,
Tomorrow fills itself with my concerns.
Last week I fed on darkness in my head
Until tomorrow ate it
And was empty.

Now work is hard but
Hooks into my cheek and picks me up,
And makes me feel the iron in my blood.

I would prefer tomorrows
Without hooks or hunger.

⊠ I can remember what my mother wore.
I knew that she was leaving and went on to school,
Pretending nothing happened.

She visited,
Sometimes my father hid these visits.
I'd been at school,
The door had closed before I opened it,
I couldn't hear her footsteps as I ran.
This was his act of kindness.

She would cry that she had left him,
And I listened, couldn't tell my father,
Nor tell her how my father was in pain,
Though both asked questions.

Now I would wish not to see my father again
If he were happy, and my mother,
Growing old in an always foreign country —
The refuge never home but better than another,
Still feels she's not arrived.

I cannot hope for footsteps with no meaning,
Nor want a noise which means I sleep in peace
And never hear the footsteps to the door.
I worry at the cost of waking late,
In ignorance of knowing what I missed,
All I know is waking wears me out,
And time's the cost I can't control or count.

A woman walked away from her small child,
And both are inconsolable.
So leave it.
The movement's not our will,
It happens anyway.

⌘ 1. I could select some furniture to stand against
A future filled with no one in particular
I could praise wood, could praise my work.
Well, I burn in work to earn some paper,
Paper for energy, paper for wood.

2. I have not spent myself on furniture.
I light small fires and throw on sticks.
Each fire is small,
Each journey takes my energy.
I am afraid to walk in the dark between small fires
Where fuel is urgent.

3. Furniture would stand,
And ones who stay so long
Their faces are habitual.
I see them rise against the wall and leave.
It is the colour of the wall I can decide.

4. The walk is not enough to keep me warm.

⌘ Sometimes moving in my sleep I touch you half-awake,
And warm, you turn in gentle motion, take my hand,
Or hold me in a touch so light it lasts through sleep.

These half-remembered wakings — as though
Lying in grass I find the sun still hot
And turn to dream of islands where the sun will always shine,
Or nudged by waves that roll beneath my back,
I hear the cries of people on the beach
Then feel the sea return.

I want to wrap you round me like a shawl,
And ease through dreams and spin out sleep
so fine and strong we never come undone.

CAROLINE HALLIDAY

*I was born on 4th July, 1947, and now live in South-east London. In between I
have been divorced, worked as a social and community worker, been involved in
Women's Aid.*

*About two years ago I wanted to write more/started to look at writing as a
feminist and became part of a women's writers group at the end of 1977. With
this group of women I began to question 'standards, methods', all male, and to
like what I wrote more, as well as seeing more clearly the political function of
writing, and of the language we use.*

*Women as friends, women as lovers, as sisters, workers, mothers; putting women
first, this is what feminism really means. It has meant becoming a lesbian and
acknowledging that means to be 'outside' sciety. It has also meant loss, of
friends, homes, and the necessity of subverting (when I can) patriarchal attitudes,
methods. At the moment it means working part-time in order to have time for
myself, for writing, and later (I hope) having a child.*

Confession

The steering wheel pressing into my back.
So I sat there, he's an uncle really.
It was the kind of hard, slimey feeling of his tongue.
The taste, and prickly, too.

They stand over you, and make you eat it, at school.
You have to go through with it.
No explanation.
Praying it will be over soon.

Confession, going to confession.
Taking me in the car.
Fasting three hours. Eating won't work for getting out of it.
If I tell . . .
Him, he's the priest. He said "Love", then he said,
"Don't tell".

Do my parents do it? How could they pretend
its nice. God made it that way.
And their room smells of bed, warm,
musty, dirty. Like sheets.
I don't like it.

You just have to.
You just have to.

When you're grown up, you want to,
you feel different.
It trickles up inside you, climbing.
Not inside me. Up to your chest — making you all dirty.
Inside — the man puts it there, and it climbs and grows.
Never do it. I'll never do it.

                    Is this me, or am I the mother,
                    or the lover?

The car stops, it is so hot, I wait
before asking, can I open the window.   Yes.
He looks glum.   Woods, fields.
If I ask why, he'll be surprised.   Maybe it's clear why.
What, I don't know.
A car's coming. Why, why are we here?
He says, 'Are you happy?' Nothing. No, I'm not,
how can I say it.
He says come and sit there. Where? I move,
I can't move right. There's no room there. I can't.

His hand on my arm, on my knee.
He says, 'I'm going to kiss you'.

> The river is flat, glassy, slight mist
> under the bridges, as the car passes.

> As she said it, I saw a child, its face screwed up,
> face in hands, saying,
> "What was I supposed to do? He was our priest,
> wasn't he?
> Friend of the family, almost an uncle. I liked him,
> even.
> He explained things well."

When he kissed me my eyes stayed open. His hair a bit greasy.
His skin looks old.
He is hard, he pushes, back, back.
I hope my back won't break, I could go to hospital.
The wheel hurts my shoulder, and my back hurts.
Where to put my hands. Wait, wait.

It stops. Look out of the window quickly, not to see eyes.
I'm going to kiss you again.
Then he tells me to sit back.
He gets out saying, "Don't look", and goes away.

Eyes tight shut, head in hands, and don't look,
don't think,   don't think,
don't pray. Tunes, that part of a hymn, where.
I hum tunes in my head.
What is he doing? I am not there. Not have to
think about.
Tunes mixed with sounds, mother and father.
I want to . . . I want to know.
Mazes, mazes. Blood in the head.

Where to walk to? I can't get back. He'd
pick me up. He'd be cross. It must be four o'clock.
I have to take gym shoes tomorrow.
Door opens. Look out of window.
Car starts.

> Sweating, she won't go on tubes.
> Panicking, she won't be alone.
> Those moments.
> No one speaks, and no questions.

56

I was staying with friends.
Downstairs a makeshift bed.
Pretext of getting a book, he arrived, semi-dark,
beside me. Leaning over, sudden kiss finding my mouth,
hands pressing my shoulders.
If I shout we're both guilty.
Would I leave tomorrow? Struggle, remonstrate. He laughs,
kisses me again, leaves.

Uncles kiss one under the mistletoe.
Family laugh, a sister grimaces.
Fathers of friends take one's hand for longer than necessary,
when no one's looking.

And the first real kiss is a surprise, a delight,
and a disgust.

Arriving back, I rush upstairs.
Voices in the hall. Did you have a nice
time? Calling me down. He drinks tea.
Take father the biscuits.
Father the hypocrite.

The weak, needy father. Only one afternoon drive, he wants to
say mass specially for you. Doesn't have family life.
He enjoys your company. Its the least you can do. The least.
I can do.

> Said nothing till I was 24.
> Told my sister not to go alone, though.
> Didn't tell her why.

Reading 'Of woman born' by Adrienne Rich.

This chapter is about pain.
Or is it about labour?
Work/birth,
worn hands, or
the farmed body of a woman.
I do not want to read this future of mine,
beautiful contusion of pain.
The hidden thought beneath the skin.

Anger is the final pain.
'Birth as affliction', not as challenge.
Will I look in fury at the man,
at the lights, dismissive faces,
clean metal,
or towards the child?
The child, firing or submerging the imagination.
Who turns to lock me in?

> 'Dreaming, I manage proudly,
> the naked child, wrapped in a towel —
> the stacks of clothes I have ready —
> of all sizes —
> and, I recall now, the child was male.'

Last time menstruation was dangerous.
Pain followed by nausea.
Nausea by fainting.
Daylight disappearing behind the wall.
Stunned and waiting for the rhythm,
the desperate rhythm, to pass.
'The woman waiting.'
A bruise spreading over the brain.

Contractions ordered by my own brain.
Startled synapses, unwilling.
Overwhelmed me with surprise for something
not felt for fourteen years with such intensity.
Or irritation at this weakened body,
a woman's.
Desire for this to be a last time,
to expand the uterus with different thoughts.

The child
its connections with death
death of the mother giving birth
the lifelong anemia of her devotion.
The child
remaining after death
pushing the line down time
after the startling body has minimised its struggle,
without asking.
I will not give up surprise.

"To change the experience of childbirth means to change women's relationship
to fear and powerlessness, to our bodies, to our children:"
Children are not beautiful.
How many children and mothers have I known?
A profound change of my life.

Your dream

I have no right to
interpretation. Your dreams are so
powerful — they terrify.
A ziggurat, you said,
(frightened of heights). And what did I do,
I said, to frighten you?
(Fearful to hear).
Steep slate sides.
We climbed and balanced,
almost exhilarated.
We meet at the edge of fear,
often. Like the night before.
You cried then, as we had passed each other
in the sheering of our fantastic minds.
I held my breath,
wondering, as we both came back,
if I was lying to you.
And if we continue all we can promise each other
is another step, and another dizzying drop.

turkish bath

bodies joined like tubers
                    breasts   thighs   bellies
                                    hot-dew covered bulbs

we are many shapes   alone with ourselves
hunched
ribbed   forming   slow   flesh
                                    falls
                                        like
                                            lava
bellies pregnant with age   misuse.
Plaiting our hair up   ebony Romans   poised in showers
unconscious queens   Smiles
at the cold plunging   Reflections
minuted in the pool   Lamps   to ourselves alone
caressing   flesh with powders   creams
                            softly nursing limbs
like children.
They chat   She took no notice
                What the doctor said before she died   Her heart.
Tall models
            unnecessary breasts hung like small sacks of sweetmeats

bikini triangles round

fragile pale hair between fair thighs
                    buttocks like sand humps
                    patted into shape   by children.

Hugeness of breasts
                    breasts as unlike as pears   and apples
                        daffodil bulbs   and crocuses.

Heat
    crisping flesh beneath
                    the skin
                        drips behind the thigh
                                    seeking
                    folds and creases like snakes.

Soap tightening already-clean-ness

flesh gradually restoring
an everyday quality as the
air thickens
　　　　　and dusts itself back into
pores
　　　　　and on the outside
carbon monoxide
heavy noises.

November, '77

In my dream I moved
between two locked parts of a bank,
through the public section.
I cannot go on labelling these parts of myself.
One shoulder, and another.

　　　Your voice regrets my need
　　　for times of solitude, to take myself into gaps,
　　　not pressing my face to your body.

　　　The dog is guiltily asleep on my cushion.
　　　The rain allows me to stay in.

The police have developed special forms of tapping.
Lasers which bounce conversations back from windows.
Do not convey messages on the phone.
(When will we, two women, feel the first sharp of prejudice?)
One in ten of the population is on police files.

　　　There are sounds of a child's violent sobbing
　　　over the fences.
　　　There are sounds of shouting.
　　　A friend knocks piercingly.
　　　Having to be honest
　　　is the real invasion, my irritation welling up.

"So that if poets insist on . . . an accurate depiction of people's
lives, as they are actually lived . . . this is a political act."

　　　There are sounds of an ice cream van
　　　groaning round the streets.

And there I was, quarter to midnight,
at the top of her house,
this woman I hardly knew,
(and I wanted to avoid involvement this week,
and write)
her husband on the doorstep,
in the phone booth,
pathetic, an empty sheet,
wanting to come in,
despite court order.
She refuses to call the police,
though he is pathetic, though he is
dangerous.

> And the child is still groaning,
> a nauseous noise.

In the raid that followed I raised my hands,
considering the outcome
of single-handed heroics.

"Illegal or violent acts provoke the state. To defend
the factories against the armed forces, the workers
will have to be armed."

I want to have plants in my room.
With a short hair cut you cannot be grabbed by the hair.

CHANDRA MASOLIVER

I'm 36. I stopped writing poetry when I was first married, and re-started when i joined the women's movement and a women's writers group. They are inextricable. I have two boys, Yashin and Ilya, and am a psychotherapist.

I am alone when
I find myself unexpectedly alone
none of my friends are in
there is no book to get on with
and I do not feel like doing anything;
then this gap wells
and if there's no warm red wine
to turn anguish to beauty,
then there's really nothing to do about it,
wait until it deadens,
dead anguish doesn't lessen
anguish, listening to it might loosen
but not lessen.
In a dream I went down a steep path
with my son, and as I turned to tell him
to be sure to shut the gate behind him
I saw him jump off the cliff.
I must really learn to comfort myself
a little better than this.

⊠   oh the
      fragments of the rain
      and the
      lost hand's touch,
      not where the finger pokes —
      explanations.

⊠   If you make time the details of the day,
      Let free-born child be monster, and your man,
      Fixed entities demanding croon and cringe,
      Then you may lose the wind through bare branches,
      Treading passages of no direction.
      If I could tell you of the child I was.
      But that got changed with marriage, turned to fusion,
      Here the rain slings you into other shapes.
      I would not lose its magic til it's lost.
      Then think what stone — still or moving — clings round
      Your face, cracking into definition.
      Dull diary. Dance and circus not your own.
      I do not wish to be the things I am.
      There's no finding that way out. Not where the
      Mind stops. Blocked, blotchy. Mouth stuffed with earth. So
      Take the flight to flower and rock dissolving.
      The partition lies in where to find it.
      Look for piper piping tunes of breaking
      Water on empty beaches, elusive;
      Some people telling in their words; Some books;
      The kaleidoscopic cracks and shadows
      In the mind, touch of tenderness, and the
      Waiting and listening alone — it's there.

◰ Walking along the green carpeted corridor
in my own house (I am alone)
I am aware of extending myself,
not the slow stretch of the lioness in the sun
nor the sharp young virgin reaching for stars
but the point of stillness the slow tilt open
finding myself there and in my dusky
green carpeted yellow walled flower filled
corridor. This is not in praise of the
solitary bird who suffers not
for company not even of its own kind.
It is nearer to knowing that I, woman,
who finds herself living this life and
having done some things well and many
badly — assessment of someone surely
full of the mystery of where her feet take her
of where hands push away and eyes lean towards,
with clear eyes I can also gather and hold
the still point the balance of myself
walking this corridor at this moment
unfolding neither outward nor inward
where light slants and dust dances.

◰ Oh the pressures of a sea-change
underneath the mind,
undergoing, unknown.
Phantom childhood
bursts out from
blue glass bell-jar
the dumb scream heard,
sudden.
we were not listening
to what we said.

I have felt myself not loved
and somewhere in this sweet world
I pay back very hard.
but if I choose to dream
of a man playing cards
not knowing what he plays
placing them easily on the table,
drunk, majestic and much loved,
to tell of my
grimy, dog-eared, greasy,
rotting anger, raucous squawk,
and rumbled troubled roar
in this thin light of concentrated hatred, cards,
then, where is the truth in my life and my feeling
and who am I paying and loving and hating
among all these people I have chosen to love and to live with?
shall I pack my bags and go and do the quick and angry act,
turn mutterer, for fear rules that kettle of fish,
the stinking kippers of my sea? no.
what are we trying to do and to say with our lives?
surely here is the home of the half light,
surely we do not yet know, no.
a long search back through a twisted mother
and the wine of peace that turned sour in my dream,
uroboros that became a snake with her coiled lips twisting
round me and my life and my hands.
not blame placed squarely on twisted tree,
but a long line to be broken,
my woman friends, and me,
women and mothers and daughters,
mixing our names to be free,
our sour wine, poor growth,
lost seasons, seeking.
we shall come through,
to a line of loving.
I shall come through,
and for me it is now.

COLLEEN ANTONIA PATTERSON

Born in the foreground of the Drakensburg mountains in October of 1944, I still cannot altogether reconcile autumn with Libra. It is only when I reflect that a southern spring lacks the surge and bursting-forth of the northern spring that I understand I am also autumn's daughter. I have a particular affinity with autumn leaves, and love not less the splendid reds, oranges, mauves of the m'sasa leaves unfurling in the spring of a savannah landscape. I love woman, plants, earth, sea, clouds, birds, mammals, streams, rocks, rainbows, . . .

you see, my mother,
how tied i am to you.
they say life and death
are inseparable
i say your pain
and my pain
are inseparable.

you see how it is.
no, you never wanted
that. no, i never
wanted that. but it
is so.

and i have no answers
and i do not know
for your pain has crippled me.

we rarely touched at all.
once i met her at heathrow
saw this small grey-haired
woman glancing anxiously
around, raised my newspaper
to catch her glance, walked
quickly to the exit. we
hugged briefly, she swallowed
several times trying to stop
the tears. i relieved her
of her luggage, guided her to
the woking bus.
she is my mother and she lets
me do things for her.

she believed in my strength
later she found that i am
not strong. still, now,
she lets me carry her luggage
and track down the right trains
and order the drinks and would
never suggest that i am anything
but strong except she rarely
speaks of her pain to me.

 to those women not fighting:

i am not afraid of you
i know the worst you can do.

you, however, are afraid of me
my worst is unknown to you.

when i say to you
"you have no need to fear me"
you become confused, frightened,
as though my fighting for you
in your absence
is some kind of madness.

— and perhaps you are right.

⊠ your coolness touches me
i put on another pullover
it is winter now.
we bring out our duffles
and our gloves
never thinking to keep
each other warm.

the purge gains momentum
there is a real sickness
seeping through our air
a sickness we breathe
out that others may
breathe in. there is
a sickness in the world
today.

your coolness touches me
i pull on my woollen hat
it is winter now.
ladybirds cluster
under leaves,
in the bark of trees,
sharing warmth.

DEB SYMONDS

*i was born in 1951 after several miscarriages and a lot of des. my mother knows
more about this than i do. i grew up in a mill town, a lake, and a slick suburb, all in
new england and more or less in that order, although the lake seems to overlap
everything else. in college my thesis tutor told me he thought of me as a visiting
savage & its taken me years to realize how this is true: in scotland, in graduate
school, still growing up, i realized that the lesbian is other, having defined herself
out of every role, living in the unknown and having a hard time describing it: here
i am, in new york, in love, in a war zone.*

didn't all the english romantics drown in the mediterranean or
lake geneva?
hiking back and forth like ants to greece,
italy, switzerland,
and seldom home.
presumably their trunks were full of important
papers.

mary shelley had had two miscarriages on the shore of lake geneva by 1818. she
was 21. percy drowned in the gulf of spezia in 1822, leaving her to support the
surviving child, percy, through harrow and cambridge by her writing: c.f. *Rambles
in Switzerland and Germany.* in 1840 sir timothy shelley acknowledged their
legitimacy and made percy his heir. later she died.

one night peggy asked me if i was a romantic
and i said no, no, that's about endings
i didn't say
do you mean the part about things we haven't done yet?

in 1849 after the death of a friend with whom she had lived for many years,
fredrika bremer toured england and america. she then went home to sweden to
work on her schemes for the emancipation and advancement of women.

look up the word: conversation.
it never used to mean talking.

a short song for the mysterious peggy lynn katz,
text without music:
you can drive through spofford wondering if i'm in the house
i'll think of you when i'm around washington st.
but today in brattleboro
this woman selling ice cream —

i will describe the wind.
i will describe in detail what has not happened between us, because
these are the things i cannot forget.
— the woman in brattleboro had your eyes)

look up the word: conversation.
you will find that it means to cohabit
to be at home
to know.

⊠ waking
to see the sun
through your curly hair,
which is also asleep;
the light rests on me
and i consider how the sunlight and your sleep are
qualities of relay and connection,
and speak to each other
while your settled head and my shoulder
exist in no relationship
now that i, the arm under your head,
am awake.
your quiet face continues
trusting last night,
not me. once i called you

some stray prince;
as you wake you can change the light on your face
by will alone, wary.
waking again
a month later
surprised to see how your full body tapers
like a boy's;
either sleeping or still
on your left side, facing the wall.
slowly leaning against your back
i would hang my arm over you
wondering what goes on between you & the wall
and spread my fingers between your breasts.

9.15 monday night, dinner. F(ather) is off in kitchen, staring into and lit by refrigerator, singing ave maria at top voice. M(other) and D are still sitting at overlit table; rest of house is dark.

D   i think i should collect all the versions of

M   ave maria?

D   no, that saying about going

M   i really thought you were going to say ave maria

D   to hell in a rowboat, to hell in a handbasket, to hell in a bobsled, to hell in a

M   when you said handbasket i remembered how when i was little we took baths in those oval (descript. handwaving) metal tubs; i was thinking that i'd really rather go to hell in one of those.

D   to hell in a tin tub?

M   yes,

D   (yelling to be heard over approaching noise) like going over niagara falls?

F walks through, still singing, carrying a carton of milk. stops, speaks to D:

F   monadnock, manognack, (confused) monognack. Your mother said one of those today.

M   it comes to me naturally.

72

☒ peggy
welds things
peggy
sleeps in a tent near her sculpture
peggy
wearing only
a black bowler white overalls gold sneakers
peggy
dances real good
peggy
carefully
calls them all boys
and calls us women
peggy
chain smoking
at 3 a.m.
finally says
hey can i kiss you

☒ my aunt caroline gave me a gold ring
when i was six
she was wearing blue jeans and an orange t shirt
sitting half way up the stairs
where they turned at a right angle
and i wanted to say shit your children will be lucky.
she was a nurse early in the mornings
coming home with stories
smoking too much
painting occasionally
driving a yellow wooden panelled beach wagon
these were the fifties, when most cars were black.
she brought me clothes from new york
which i rarely wore
and taught me to driver her next car, the yellow chevy,
down the driveway
the first thing i ever said was
"caroline got her transmission fixed"
when i was twelve she married and
i wore a purple dress and ran off to go swimming
and people remarked because they weren't the sort
to recognize me wet.
three years ago she gave me an old ring of hers
a very worn cameo,
the lady's head keeps falling out.
so, furies.

you excellent young women
you excellent old women
write me another pamphlet
because i saw a smartass young woman
stacking her paintings against the refrigerator
and her children see an invalid
bleeding tranquilly in a chair
bleeding her way out.
she is a nurse, she is clever, this is a translation.
her vagina is always bloody now
her friend, as they say, is with her.
knowing that all women do not recover to bleed again,
write me another pamphlet
i have bought half a dozen for her
i have tried buying dozens
and my friends don't need any more.
let me explain that i want to buy her roses.

⊠   her hands
goddammit her hands were like two rocks
and when she hit a new country
the first thing she would buy were pens
cheap biros, bics, pentels, pilots
that rattled with the money in her pockets;
and she wrote on her hands:
this is a message for women who play guitars
for women seeing women play guitars —
watch the left hand,
silent
a spider in her web,
moving.
take alix dobkin's left hand for example.
stick the plastic on the machine;
in the timing, the gaps, the bass pulse,
i hear that left hand
wrist, ligaments, fingers
describing both time and the distance they must move;
and behind the music is the silent arrogance
of women whose hands speak now.
we will take language back to the body:
this is a message for women whose hands
learn their music from the muscles of the vagina
the solar plexus
the throat.

DIANA SCOTT

Born in 1947 and lives in Leeds. Trained in Drama and Teaching English as a foreign language, her present commitments are building work, co-operative living and working and literature. She is beginning work on an anthology of women's poetry for Virago. She is a large person with a reputation as an intellectual. She is very intuitive and quite witty.

Poem for the Dark Goddess. on the full moon

The full moon
fills the midnight street with dawn light
like water
A silver night:
Dawn on a dead through terrace —
the women are mad.
Their hollow bones fill with ice and light.
They will kill and eat.
They have seen the smoke rising from their own bodies.
They have woken in the mixed flare
of moon light and street glare
to the scream of their own bodies
burning.
they have said
we always knew —
we were betrayed
our wombs were ripped

promises were made to us
they were never kept —
we always knew
that the women were right
right in our despair,
right in our rage,
right in our justice,
right in our self-betrayal
and we are coming
on quiet unhurrying feet
our hands stretching
our eyes staring
we are coming to claim our justice

Do not plead ignorance
or goodwill
It will not save you
The women will rip you
like the paper of your empty contract
and eat you.
Their bodies will fill up with peace
like the swimming moon
They will sleep in the watery dark
and wake calmed.
This will happen
again and again.
Their rage will never be used up.
neither will their justice.

OF THE CHILDREN OF OTHER PEOPLE.

I.

I am in control of my own life
the new mother said
meaning, I own a child,
and can control her
So, she had said, this child-fish
holds the secret.
a secret heart pulsing against my huge palm
a small vein pulsing
at the crown of
the still open skull

the fingers of each curled fist
suck on their own thumbs
The eyes are open
a small anus
flowers with shit
urine arches or seeps
from a folded, secretive cunt
She felt that she owned life
now she had made a child
blood of the dark solstice descends her
rope of growth
into an unliquified, airy world.
I am in control of my own life
she said
meaning I own a child
and can control her
to make up for the fact I am not free

2.
I am in control of my own life
the childless woman said
meaning I am free
knowing at the back of her mind
she was talking nonsense
(for who is free in a
world where all free choice is mapped out
before our children are born
and free free choice rocks mountains?)
I am responsible only to myself
What is myself if
not my life?
What is my life if not the
miracle gift of knowing
that being is?
Most women discover this only in childbirth,
she conceived,
but I am giving birth to myself
as all sisters should nowadays —
feeling the children of the other women
curled like petals in their prams
as a blow to the hollow in the heart
but carrying on.
I am in control of my own life
the childless woman said
meaning I am free . . .
. . . possibly . . .

Six poems for hospital workers

1. This is a poem for
the hospital orderly
who does the waterjugs
serves the breakfast
serves the tea
gives out the menus
serves the coffee
cleans the lockers
collects the menus
serves the lunch
serves the tea
serves some more tea
and clocks off
Next morning she starts the whole thing again —
does the water jugs
serves the breakfast . . .
This poem is boring.
It gets boring, after eleven years, she says.

2. This is not a woolworths waitress
(or is it)
This is a nurse in
the new national uniform
Little boy blue gingham and
a paper hat.
She gets electric shocks making the
new kings fund beds.
Changing babies nappies would be better
she thinks, stowing disposable bed pans
at least they don't shit so much
all at once

3. These are the kitchen workers
wearing disposable hairnets
and stifling long sleeved polyester overalls.
They rest on boxes in their basement corridors
Why are they so hot, the kitchen workers?
Unlike everywhere else in this brand new hospital
There's no air conditioning in the kitchen
that's why they're so hot
Why are they looking at the thermometer,
those kitchen workers?

When the external temperature reaches 80f
They don't have to fry or bake — food that is
they go on regardless
Why are there so many middle class Ugandan asian kitchen workers?
for example —
You ask too many questions
Let's get on to the next poem

4. This is a poem for
the dying woman
who is going
who is not here
who is
who is
silence for the dead woman
who is completed now
Her blood flows to the back of her head
The round globe of her face
is ascending
Her body, in its disposable shroud
is waiting
for the polythene wrapping
for the two labels
for the black wooden box on wheels
careering to the mortuary
past the day shift going home.

5. Cleaning under this bed is
the married woman sociology student
who is working all through her vacations
as she doesn't get a grant
(her husband works all through his vacations
as a porter
and gets 30% more)
She has noticed with excitement
how nobody looks at cleaning women
or respects them
Nobody looks at students pretending
to be cleaning women either
(they don't join unions)
Everyone notices her accent
She talks loudly because her husband never listens
"Aren't you rather educated to be a cleaner, cleaner?"
they ask her constantly.
"Oh, you're a student."
She's going to put it all in her disseration

She can't imagine how people who
work there always
put up with it
She gave in her notice today, gratefully
after ten weeks

6. Here is a poem for
the women who don't write poems
who do the work because work is
and do more work because work is
who are: fast, kind, vacant, fat
service and produce, produce and service
There are no words to write this poem because
they have no words.
Who would do their jobs
if they had words. No more words. The poems over.

Social Security visiting inspector semi-blues

Woke up this morning round about nine o'clock
been up three times in the night to feed the baby
and sure wasn't feeling so hot;
I looked around with gummy eyes at walls,
floor, ceiling, baby, dirty dishes from the night before,
when there's a knock
and it's the Social Security visiting inspector
coming in through my door.

"We never come unannounced," he says.
"Not even at four in the morning: we always knock.
There's no *man* hiding under your bed, dear Miss Object?
Good; I didn't mean to give *you* a shock.
So kindly remove the excrement from that chair,"
he says to me,
"and I'll sit down and ask you a lot of extremely personal questions
dear Miss Case
If you co-operate it'll be over quite quickly
you'll see."

"(excuse me I can see your titties, dear Miss Boobs
kindly feed your infant later, I can't concentrate
on putting you down,)"

"Now tell me dear young unmarried mother
Miss Fallen Woman," he says to me with a frown,
"What's the birthday of your child
and when were you born
and who was your next of kin?
Was it your father or your mother
your sister or your brother?
Who put it to you?
Who put it in?

We're keeping tabs on you
We're keeping tabs on you
We want to know the father of your child
Tell us the names of all your friends
their addresses — it never ends
So we can trace you wherever you go
Tell us the number of your doctor
the number of your car
the name of your solicitor
you'll need one when we're through with you —"

"Tell us the father of your child, his name
and his address, his occupation —
I hope he's a good earner
So he can make an honest woman of you
and get you off our hands
and look after you as a real man should!
. . . now tell me dear Miss Legs,
how many times, and on this bed?
You obviously need someone to look after you?"

Got the SS shakes, I could hardly say a word,
It's not funny when they're doling out the pennies,
but I knew what's what, *and what I needn't say*
so I didn't, and he couldn't and in the end he went away,
and I said, any babies of your own, by the way
and he blushed and said "Miss Dropout
I'm only married six months
no way, got to save for the car, for the wife . . .

. . . time is flying!" So he flew!
and I knew
            they may be keeping tabs on me
                                    Mr Inspector

but
not
like
on
   you!
        They're keeping tabs on you
        They're keeping tabs on you!

A LOVE POEM TO MYSELF

Feeling.
We wrote much love poetry.
We responded sensitively to nature.
We wrote other things.
Ignored. Suppressed. Unpublished.
Feeling.
Feeling our way in the dark
without room or language.
Feeling.
I don't want to write poetry about feeling.
I know how I'm feeling.
Bloody terrible.
I can't write poetry glorifying my heart,
my heart pretty dried up,
battered, cracked, full of rubbish
from a world I don't own.
I can't write poetry glorifying my mind
my mind educated to think and speak
in the Man's language
How can I glorify my body, battered and stretched,
turned thirty now,
aches beginning,
a bad back, a caesar cut —

But I will praise
my wit
my strength
my height
that I have made
that I will make
that I respect the dark

that I know how to love
and I will praise the
power of the word in woman
saying it over and over
wim-min . . . wim-min . . .
and remembering or dreaming
women stamping and dancing and chanting
wim-min . . . wim-min . . .
but what more we have no idea for the words are lost
and yet the room lifts up
the long serpent rippling through bone
and blood and skin
and explodes
And they shout until their voices die away
and the roof comes back on the room
which comes back to women . . .
This have I done for my true love
and this have they done for us, for us . . .
Now they are going out of the dancing room, slowly
their voices are working with power

The great voice of one filling the hall and
stairwell
Their great voices resonate the building
like a pipe for the wind
The girl children come out to listen
They look at the women with great eyes, silently
What is going on their eyes are asking
Soon the girl children will know what is going on:
And dreaming or remembering this I know
I have written a poem of
feeling, women, together
coming
towards
me.

GILL HAGUE

*My paid work has been in community work/social work/youth work type jobs
ever since I was employed as a community organiser in the co-operative daycare
movement in North America in the late sixties. In fact, I was deeply involved in the
social and political explosions of those times and they shaped my political formation
formation. Thus I became a committed and active socialist several years before I
became involved in the Women's Movement. I have been active in the socialist
feminist part of the Women's Movement since 1973, have been working on a book
about adolescent women and have had a few poems published in various places.
I've always written poetry — since I was about 7 apparently. I have a baby daughter
and live with her father and two other people.*

The Well-Balanced People

Still, I hear them,
the well-balanced people,
talking, joking,

caught within their frameworks.
They are easy to pity.
I have shut them out;

no time at all for superficial chatter.
Like boomerangs,
my splinters

shoot around me.
Such sharp arrows;
they hurt the eyes like fireworks.

I am mesmerized;
yet always interrupted.
My barricades, you see, are badly built,

and still I hear them,
the well-balanced people.
They graze my surfaces; I must take care.

(If it gets half a chance,
my female guilt
will glue up all the splinters.)

Uncertainty

Inside me,
a great question-mark
with barbs to make me feel hasty.

Too hard to conceive
that the question-mark will
become

a real baby,
will brazenly snap my stamina.
A brave face

is what I have,
falsely of course,
to put on it.

How confident,
how poised, oh yes,
while the grey-green fear

washes over me,
swirling about my ankles.
And the panic

wants to rise and can't
because of solid discipline,
of old poetic ways.

Both of us,
we look through my eyes,
but what we see right now is darkly.

Confused, like wraiths,
we waft through the mists
fingers-crossed for solid ground.

For a Housewife

Woman at home
I am,
clamped between these walls;
a subtle press, this one,

whitening red fingers
round lone coffee cups.
Uncombed hair and cloistered.
Uncombed hair? Who cares?

My mind's become amorphous,
sliding like quatermass
and splintered by these chores,
this house, my castle. Fragments.

See them draped on this cupboard,
dusted under that bed.
Busy bits of jelly.
A rare sight in a man's world.

You'd better be sure and notice;
up there in that child's room,
my precious screaming brain-cells,
hung up by their feet,

like fish out of water.
Oh water, give me water.
Of course, shades of wastelands,
but on the other hand,

such comfortable wastelands.
They fester under carpets
like overlooked infections.
Tell me how do you get gangrene?

(Well anyway, I always say,
day after day, I always say,
it'll be alright for sure
when they all get home tonight.)

Three/one women

I
Here is a woman for you;
always moving on to something else;
(interpret that as you will).

II
Here is a woman for you;
trying to be alone with the wild-plants.
Can you not allow her that?

III
Here is a woman for you;
she is sufficient unto
herself.

GILLIAN ALLNUTT

I think that the task for women now is to reject all the definitions of ourselves that have been offered/forced upon us by men and to re/discover and say who we are. I have chosen to discover and say myself through writing, and the poems and stories I come up with are my contribution to this collective and individual task. I decided to 'be a writer' at the age of 11, but it is only in the last two years (I am now 29) that I have had the confidence to say so and to try and do it full time (keeping teaching and typing, my money-makers, to a minimum). I have been involved in the Poetry Workshop at the Women's Arts Alliance for over two years now and find it an invaluable source of support and constructive criticism and a place where I can really share writing which is otherwise a rather isolated occupation.

THE TALKING PRINCESS

I should like to have been a sleeping beauty,
but I woke
and begged one question of my adoring prince.
Would he accord my dream reality?
I spoke
and have not slept since.

IMAGES OF REVENGE

I am the nude
who dresses beneath
her skin.

I am the smile
that hollows
the dimpled chin.

I am the eye
that lowers
the fluttering lash.

I am the soul
that seduces
your fragile flesh.

I am the hole in the dyke
where your finger
gets stuck.

I am the deluge (apres toi)
that will drive you
into the ark.

I am the whale
that swallows the hook and the line
and the man.

I am the black hole
that has sucked in
the sun.

HARRIET ROSE

Publications — The Steel Circle, Belladona, Crotchless Knickers and Fifteen Hail Marys (forthcoming). Widely published in magazines and anthologies: PEN, Arts Council, Bananas, Ambit, Tree, Confrontation, Gallery, Contemporary Women Poets, etc. Writes novels and was in women's poetry theatre with The Prodigal Daughters. Is a feminist despite her dislike of isms and is impressed with the barriers that the movement has broken down between women such as the fictional media generated generation gap; but doubts whether she herself can ever be acceptable as one of a group or work collective being basically an isolate and uneasy in group situations.

THE LOST PRINCESS

"Below that wall on Famine Street
There is nothing left but the heart to eat"
Edith Sitwell

And the heart is eaten.

We are singing canticles in the slaughterhouse
And we are singing singing
and the roads heave up beneath us
and the words of God are breathing
down our spines.

Below the rock vaults piled up
the night wind shook shook shook.
And with its force your grandma's house
is shaken
Belladona.

"My legal name
is a red coloured paper heart
they had pinned to my dress.
They said I had to have one"
wrote Belladona as she closed her eyes
thinking of her grandma's house in Brooklyn
and Fat Helen leaning out the front window
shouting "Flora Flora"
"Flora's playing jump rope
with her cousin Filene."

And the tide's left eye
sank to the shape of her wrath
and they all filed past
dancing in procession.
"Belladona, Belladona"
they all cried "we will eat you,
we will eat you, we will eat you up alive."

Below the smells of laundry boiling
at the Ching Ching Ching Chinaman's
and the smokey air where food is cooked
she sat on the curbstone
where old men
waiting for glimpses of her grandmother
who did not look old
gave her El Producto cigar bands
to wear as rings around her fingers
all too big.

And there were rings on her fingers and bells on her toes
And there was Mommy singing into the heavy baby carriage
and Belladona dancing to the television
and music blaring on the radio.

"And Grandmother had no heart" they said
"It was all cut up when she was sent from home at sixteen
so her older sisters could marry."
She was sent on a cruise around the world
and lived in many cities.

Her name on paper was Rebeccah.
But the old men whispered "Tamar".
And on Friday midnight
under the simple light of a low burning taper
she told Belladona
"whatever your name is
they will call you Tamar."

And there were rings on her fingers
and bells on her toes
and Mexican castanets as small as her fingers
to dance round the tar covered roof
and Tirzah, the Shekinah, with flames in her red hair
came out of hiding
the prophet Ezra roaring in the grate.

And on the day her grandma died
the house was shaken
and an ancient Hebrew princess
marked her forehead
with soot from the streets
and wailed clutching fencepost and pavement.
And the brutal boy from around the corner
the bad boy who played with Flora and Filene
came and kicked and hit her with his fists
and touched her nose with a tiny bird
he'd stoned to death.
"Georgy Georgy" called his mother out the window.
"Flora Flora" called Fat Helen.
And small and birdboned Belladona
was lifted in her mother's arms
unable to stop crying.

THE FIRE ROOM

She was sitting in the fire room
when the Inquisitor came.
"There is no need for speech"
he said, taking her silence as a sign.

His face is lined now.
He is accompanied by a gap toothed old woman
with dirty bandages around her ankles.

"There have been too many depositions"
he said in a weary voice
the gap toothed woman watching
reaching for her shoulders.

She shuddered away.

      She can remember him as time lives in far memory, the Inquisitor,
his black robes burning hanging from his arms like batwings running to the
sea which became a river.

"I have superimposed the face of the Inquisitor
on your Shadow" she wrote
disintegrating
into her own uncontrolled experiments upon herself.

The fire room is a transparent globe
where there is neither up nor down
just the frogspawn face of a villain
in clerical dress, visions and burning.

It is the dark time of the year
which makes the fire room more frightening.

HELEN RAMSBOTTOM

I was born in Shipley, Bradford — which is in Yorkshire. That means a lot to me because I like to feel I still belong to the North although I haven't lived there for ten years now. I also like to think I'll go back and live there.

I started writing poems at school and was fairly well encouraged, but going to university to do "Literature" almost killed off any creativity I felt I had. Now I'm over that and writing again. I work as a printer.

Up north

We travel inter-city.

Your eyes dart across the countryside
like the carriage of a typewriter
back and forth
back and forth.

They register green flickering
hills, curves the empty flat —
changes from
South to North.

Beside me, my
golden one,
magpie dressed
in black and white.

Confident, assured, a little
sad maybe.

distant.

✠ You are
clean sheets
to me.

A correction
in red,
precision, and
all those perfect phrases
I invent in the bathroom
and promptly forget.

I'm upset
by my own tears at your memory.

Loving you hard,
fiercely as I used to
hold the reins,
scared
on horse-back,
sweeping through the wind.

✠ moaning about the bitterness
she drains her mug
and leaves the bits at the bottom,
curls up and falls asleep.

sits up, cross-legged on the bed
for writing purposes, hair down,
without her nightdress,
two rolls of fat, she is too
fat. I listen to her talk

it's all rubbish, She
can only stare out of corners,
cry over counters and whisper
names in ecstatic bliss, I
pity her sometimes
her drandruff hurts

She should be
put away

⊠ Frustration, like a damp trickle
seeps into my mind.

I have raided and rifled
your bottom drawer, beneath
piles of folders and old magazines
to read again the letters
of another lover long ago.

In the same way I
used to raid the drawer
at home; beneath
the metal box of insurance policies
lay two books, bound
in brown paper, about sex.
I read pages and pages
on the theory of orgasm,
I knew what it was
even then.

The thrill is not the same —
both demand compulsive
secret reading,
but this one hurts as
I read alone, heart beating;
does not give pleasure
but pain.

I long for the other —
it is not forthcoming.
Had you kept
sex manuals too, I might
have forgiven you.

⊠ Beethoven
shifts craftily from
one key to another,
booming confident
towards an inevitable
ending.

No
tentative feeling
searching for the flow
from black note
to note —
only the surefire blast
and harmony as
protective and soothing
as the whisper
of a tall, dark
handsome stranger.

JANE HOLIDAY

Born Deddington, Nr. Banbury, Oxfordshire. Have lived in Wigan since 1976 with my two Sierra Leonean daughters, Yewa (16) and Amanda (15). Reckon to have moved house at least 32 times and have lived (among other places) in Edinburgh, Glasgow, London, Bo, and Kenema. Have had numerous jobs including wife, cinema usherette, sheet metal worker, cake packer, waitress, bus conductor, Civil Servant and teacher. At present combine supply teaching with writing, hoping to make the latter a full-time occupation eventually. Have written three children's books and a fourth, "Biddy's Talking Pineapple" (Hodder & Stoughton) will be published next year. Have had several programmes of poetry on Radio Blackburn and contributed poems to BBC Radio 3 ("The Northern Drift") and BBC Radio 4 ("Just After Noon") as well as being a regular contributor to "Lancashire Life". I particularly value being included in this anthology.

MARYSE

Did I ever tell you about Maryse?
She was a naturalised French, Spanish Jew.
We met every afternoon in Kenema showfield
When she was learning to drive.
We stopped at the same market stall always
And bought, from the disapproving Foulah trader,

A packet of High Life, a can of Star beer,
Sometimes a few oranges to suck
Or some of those greasy doughnuts
The women cooked at the roadside.

Jalloh, he was called, that Foulah
With his light brown skin and elegant nose.
Warm brown eyes caressed our children
Bundled in the back of the Peugeot,
Then flicked us over coolly.
Two spoiled white women
Taking their pleasures viciously,
Is that how he saw us?

Perhaps an hour each day we sat on those hard seats
And talked of Proust and tobacco,
Our husbands and ourselves,
Even our fingers touching drilled a nerve.
Often we just sat and watched the cows.
(Thin, unhealthy putty-looking beasts)
And then we'd speak of distant, happier times
When we'd be together without our husbands
In a remote island.

I got away from mine.

Maryse? Her husband beat her to death one night,
Jealous of those few hours spent watching cows.

DISGUISE

Like cream bulging out of a sponge sandwich,
OOzing witticisms like spots of jam,
Phrases spill out of my ears
Behind and underneath and sideways
While I am talking.

Inanities slouch from my jaws
While I listen to the words weaving webs.
Sometimes I cannot hear what my mouth is saying
For the minty word-salad of my mind.
Words have been my downfall . . .

Though I live by them. . .
Words bought this wine,
That bookshelf,
These steaks and french fries.
Words squeeze my life and suck the riches out.

JANE TILLY

I'm 25 and living in London. I grew up as the eldest of five children in a lower middle-class, suburban family — jealously hating my sister, closer at first to my brothers. Through adolescence I fought with my mother, a powerful woman, worked hard at school, "went out" with boys, and fell in love with girls.

I took a social studies degree and tried to "succeed" both academically and by having a man. But I found both things oppressive, and through lesbian feminist literature began to understand why, and to think that there may be alternatives. Since then I've become involved in the Women's Liberation Movement, and in loving and sharing living situations with women. I've struggled with various straight jobs, including teaching, and spent a year on the dole.

Writing has been one way I've tried to share and make sense of these experiences and feelings of anger, pain and love.

my brother

Well, some women tell me that you're my brother
so let me tell you
about the brother i knew best
Until i was 15 and he was 12
i was bigger and stronger and cleverer than him
but he had a few more privileges than me
so that sort of evened things out,

and we were the best of friends
sharing confidences, games, fights and seaside holidays.
I even consoled him over his first wet dreams
and showed him how to begin
to kiss and love a woman.
But then he got bigger and stronger than me,
and his mates soon taught him how
good it was to be
a powerful man.
I kept on being cleverer than him but who gave a shit
when he could always put me down with his fist.
so if you wanna be my brother, mate,
then show me your sister first.

⌘ Crazy that he still has the energy to do it
a small black boy turning cartwheels
on the dusty station platform
sun shining hot, NF slogans on the wall
crazy that i'm smiling and seeing the sun
in this city of roads, railings
torn down squats, concrete blocks
men eyeing me with hatred
hating me, hating women
trying to rape us, happy together.

some days ago
she said to me,
sharing thoughts as gentle as the
flowers i drew on her skin,
"The happiness is unjustified, but real
the struggle wears me out and alone
i miss the flowers"
oh, my love, how i wish
you could see the cartwheels in the sun
am i crazy to think i could show you?

JANET DUBÉ

As for words about myself, I may have something to say just before I die,
otherwise anyone will have to read my poems or become my friend or both.

it'll take a long time
but it will come, when
our children's children
or our children, or even
we ourselves, will look
back at these our times

and see ourselves for what we are
the bluffing bureaucrats
the track tied technocrats
the earnest freaks we have become

there's nothing sane about our lives
except the will to change it all
in every smallest part. Any
love we find or make or take
in the meantime may be
no more than we deserve

no less than we need
and still only just enough
to keep us insanely going
clock cuckoos in a world of
creatures, water, air, and life
that's wrongly wound up with us:

self sounding idiots
breaking apart with songs.

Nothing we say's to be trusted
Nothing we say's a lie.

to the man (for once)

if your ear hums and aches
    for some other beauty
as your small sharp energy
    hovers between meanings

this will no longer delight us
and we will not pretend surprise
or charm or even be polite:

and if something tells you
that we no longer know
or care what you are thinking,
that you cannot hurt us now
and that this time
nothing will be taken from us

then you are right at last.

She who slept for aeons is waking
and we are speaking in the energy
of our own meaning, which is
her life. We shall be humble enough
to learn, and we are not afraid
of knowing. We are not afraid
of being strong, and there is
nothing you can take.

Be humble enough to learn.
Be quiet.

brief for a statement to the authorities

to whom it may concern
you were alive

but to be who you were
you needed me to do your work
fulfil your plan, be happy
learn your language, know your god

to be alive
I needed work

we could not separate
each from the other
or from the task
that was between

my hands, my living strength
fulfilled your plan

there was no other plan

and for long years I learned
to speak your language

there were no other words

you went too far
and now
I am alive without you
I do not need your language
I don't fulfil your plan
or answer your questions, know your god

I am alive, and look
now, if you can see
look now, look all around
look at the grass, the grain
the corn, the ground, the growing
earth, see what is damaged
what you took of life
see what is lost

and see what language
we will learn now
we are alive without you

we are alive together
a strong familiar wordless
song unites us: now
is the time

104

⊠ I shall get stopped
I keep saying. What
do you mean, they keep
saying. I don't know.
But it's all so new.

A thousand years ago
ten thousand years ago
a hundred years ago
last month, last week,
even yesterday, I couldn't.

I kept getting stopped.
So this is very surprising.
I shall get stopped
I keep saying. Even
yesterday I couldn't do

it, and as for tomorrow
who knows. My prophecies
deal in other things
and anyway
I don't understand them.

⊠ everyone
except maybe some people
who we needn't mind now
because they wouldn't understand
anyway,

everyone
has barbed wire
around their throats. Do you
find the inside barbs more
troublesome, or the ones
on the outside, that only
tighten when you try to speak?

nod your head
by way of answer
one nod for inside, two nods
for shutup, my love, my fool
you'll make it worse.

Before the almond blossoms
on her iron boughs
what does she find to say?
how good
if that is what this means.

Before the silence of the snow
the silence of the sky. One day
around the silence of our lives
the poems of our world.

⊠   death has set no fashion
that I know of.

when I married
most of my friends
did much the same;

while I had children
most of my friends
had children;

when the rest of us
were political.
I was too;

writing — it didn't take
so long to find other people
doing it. Getting arrested
dropping out of school
the women's movement

the lovers, the raids,
the houseful of cats
and people and children

the trips; all
of my unique experience

matches something
in most of the people
I know. Everyone's
been doing it, some
of it, most of it,
whatever it is
most of the time.

death is more awkward.
the loss of a love
it's not fashionable to feel

for a life
it wasn't fashionable
to bear.

who were those mothers
our sisters

to whom it all was commonplace,
the death of a child?

where did it go
all the raw feeling,
the guilt, confusion,
madness, love,
and fear

they must've felt?

like most other things
in those days
it helped make
women women
and men men

I guess. We don't
want that, I think.
We want to be ourselves,
doing it.

I have news for us.

this raw, unfashionable
awkward love
with no place to go
is it.

that's a very strong image
that we've been going long enough
and have revealed bone. I've seen
our pain, we've seen our pain
so deep and dully aching
we might have asked to lose
an ear or eye or foot or hand
instead of what we've lost already
if anyone could offer us that choice.

But they couldn't. Being women
and known what that means
there's not much choice these days.
Being women, and not knowing
what that means, we are choosing
between struggles in which we
shall be more or less defeated
between pains that we shall
suffer if we choose or not,

between speech or silence
both of which will tell our truths
and tell our lies, for neither
speech nor silence is our own.

Perhaps we have reached bone.
Perhaps it's time for us to
sever all the nerves and ease
some piece of shin or shoulder out
from someone's restless body

wipe it clear of blood
and make it some new
singing instrument. See how
cleanly white it shines, and
that limb from which it came
hangs no more limply useless
than before. Sing sisters. Let's
hear the music of our flesh
and blood. Those who think

we're lying when we speak
won't hear our kind of singing
anyway; and we can hear
each other sing, and dance
and play and be together.

We can hear each other's silence
and make poems out of that.
We can hear each other's stories
and make silence out of that;

we can blow each other's trumpet
and get going to the sound
of all that music crashing in our ears.
We can you know. We are.

⬧ so I will dive
to depths past speech
where all the colours are:

and words like weed
trail meaningless
above my head:

I could make gifts
from all the colours
spinning, sliding
rainbow round me:

would you take a gift
from me, say red,
or maybe blue?
see how the sunlight
shines them.

we are Ophelia: laugh
or cry my dear,
for this is where we are.

JUDITH BARRINGTON

is 34, six feet tall and hates Christmas. She lives in Oregon, in the Pacific North-
west of America, with her lover and two children. On forms that demand to
know her occupation she sometimes writes "poet" but not always. She has been
actively involved in the Women's Liberation Movement in London and in
America for six years and is a radical feminist. Currently she is working on a
study of women poets as well as trying to find audiences of women to read to.
Last International Women's Day she handed copies of her poems to women in
the street.

Where are the brave new worlds
I have heard about
and dreamed about with you?
There for the taking, if only
roots and strands and
great enormous burrowing growths
of old familiar worlds
were not embedded deep within me.
Where is the freedom
which I want for you
to grow beside me and away from me?
There for the taking, but for
desperate clinging which will strangle it.

109

We cannot find it
till its hurt has bitten us
and goes on biting till we feel no more.
The brave new worlds
will not be made of words
or thoughts or visions
talked about and written down;
but, rather, they will grow
on tiny fragments of our bleeding flesh
from which we've torn out
the masses of disease.
No room, of course,
for being careful when we're tearing out.
Only hope that pieces which are needed
for survival stay intact.

COMING HOME
A Villanelle on Jealousy

Two pillows lying side by side
I wonder why they're not a single pile;
A silent movie clatters through my head.

Our candle is shorter, my cyclamen died;
You say that you missed me — after a while.
Two pillows lying side by side.

I filter the details: a train leaves its shed,
Wheels slide the rails like a worn-out file;
The movie clatters silence through my head.

Fifty miles back someone hitching a ride
Had told me "Possession's not really my style".
Two pillows lying — side by side.

I talk of the journey; one tire had no tread;
Watch for omissions; what prompted that smile?
The silent movie clatters through my head.

My questions are seething, I pack them inside,
Want to believe your unspoken denial;
Two pillows lying side by side.
A silent movie clatters through my head.

REFLECTION ON BEING TAKEN FOR A MAN

I

Public lavatories
are more trouble than they're worth
— these days
except of course in true emergencies
and then I take good care
to shape up
avoid trouble
not embarrass anyone
who might mistake me for a man
as they frequently do
— these days.
"Excuse me, but this is the LADIES"
have said old women — tentative,
younger ones — hostile,
while I cringe and mutter (falsetto)
and disappear fast when they realize
what they have done.
These days, if I must,
I enter fast
hands out of pockets
shirt buttons undone, in summer,
humming high and loud
and just for good measure
I smile.
Looking how I please in the world
was supposed to be
liberating.

II

My friends (whose raised consciousnesses
refer to different standards
from the rest of the world)
say that I'm womanly —
one of them once even said, flatteringly,
Amazonian, and I was pleased.
My reflection is unfamiliar,
bears no relation to my thoughts
and little to my history.
Mirrors confuse me
like people who say
"can I help you sir".

And the guilt that I feel when they say it
comes quicker and easier
than the glare or the smile
with which I have learned
to put them right
or put them down.

"How *did* Women's Liberation
become so confused with the
human growth movement?"
— Meg. March 5 1978

A million marching women
each with a mirror in her hand
laying bare her bowels
in an orgy of self realization.
Oriental candles sputter celebration
because we are all moving
where once we stood still,
isolated, unaware.
Awareness blooms like a tangerine sunrise —
the kind that hangs in waiting rooms,
mass produced
rainbows over Mount Hood
with a plastic pot of gold
labelled HUMAN POTENTIAL.

A million marching women
each with her own mirror,
her own marching band
and her own route, mapped out
by the mirrored image
of her personally political
unfolding soul.
Unpredictable side-trips
explode consciousness:
the mirror reflects labia,
soft woman flesh, ripe for experiment:
familiar trap, this path
to new preferences, old skills
labelled POLITICAL RELATIONSHIPS.

112

It is no accident, my friend,
that we march out of step,
hands full of soul mirrors,
hostility pillows
and each other's cunts;
eyes blind to all
but the glass vision.
It is no accident that we march
heads down; the oppressor
hands out the mirrors and smiles;
he knows we mustn't look up —
we might see how many we are;
how strong and beautiful
our numbers.

JUDITH CAREY

*I was an actress, had children, got married, came to live in Cambridge. I joined
the Women's Movement around the time of the birth of my second child in
January, 1971.*

*I remember talking about wanting to be a poet in a consciousness raising group a
year or so later — I had been writing diary type prose, but didn't keep it up at
that time. My first poem appeared in the Cambridge Women's Liberation News-
letter a couple of years later. It was a response to an article by a woman called
Carol Naughton about anti-intellectualism in the movement among other things.
Carol has subsequently become one of my best friends and our relationship has
been very fruitful for my writing.*

        ❈ Pompous in pinstripe
           the Commuter flashes
           his cheap red biro
           at the sad and snooty secretaries
           on the six twenty two
           who
           see him and see through him,
           daily.

L.A. Poem.

No way
Can I write
A laid back
Poem.

The Family Man's hands are cold
His feet have turned to clay
His bones are old
His eyes have closed
Soon he'll waste away.
He'll leave behind no legacy,
no fortune or good luck,
cos all he really cares about
is making a fast fuck.

His pretty little daughter
always says 'Yes, please,'
in case he turns his icy back
or maybe starts to wheeze.
She flatters him and coddles him
and makes him cups of tea
and props his wilting ego up
till nineteen eighty three.

His-car is his necessity.
He'll rub it till it gleams
and when he's in the driving seat
you'll know
he's what he seems.

JUDITH KAZANTZIS

Wrote 'Women in Revolt' (Jackdaws, 1968) and in 1977 a first book of poetry
"Minefield" (Sidgwick and Jackson). Contributed to "Seven Women", an
anthology from the Women's Literature Collective, and has reviewed poetry for
Spare Rib.

I've been a feminist since I argued my brothers should do the washing-up too.
Didn't win, then. Now, I write, draw, and prefer my kids as they get older.
Would have been either *Bette Davis* or *Joan Crawford* or *an explorer up the*
Amazon basin if could start again. Or all four.

towards an abortion

difficult. after ten years
of foolproof device, I'm a fool, the fooled
— and the play-capped fool.
this is the third one, second
mistake later, third pencil point
third blackberry growing
in the heart of my bushy belly,
no heart to it and foolishly.

I can pluck out fruit
eject cuckoo, erase a stipple.
yes, if I make up my mind to it.

my little girl of the gulf,
your open eyes wander all night —
you laugh at me, you have fat legs
you totter round me, your hands
to my waist, wanting to be lifted,
I'm all baby language, wanting
to get you a smocked dress, and emeralds
and a go cart for north of the wind,
to make you my chuckling sweetheart in —
you smack me a kiss, waving
your plump wrist.

yet if you bind me
you
preferring your dad

you
causing midwives, hospitals, doctors
stitches, agony

yes you, my girl, the gaiety
of antenatal clinics
the great gravid company of mothers to be
and pride swollen after
                    and chatty —
false milk, and the maddened
enlarging of two a.m. nipples
and the slouch through
sylvia's milkbottle hour
                    (where is *she*?)

yes my girl, you if you
must go through the rites of preschool play
groups, no play for me
the picking up time, and the dumping
time, the injections, the yells, the
heinz spinach on the carpet
the aching bent back
                    powdering your
bottom, my sweet, with boots zinc white
your padipad arse, your au pair
on the slave train from basle

117

knowing no english, except, swinging,
and glum in her room
                    when she doesn't

you my chuckling sweetheart, when
you will sulk and say
it's all my fault
and can't we buy a pony
and go to disneyland:
                    you if you
scowl at me and really
are better off when I'm out,
and if it's always unfair,
and intone television jingles
if I ask you to sing
                    me one song you know

and you bicker and bicker
                    and bicker
till I hit you like a G.I. and you cry;
and you talk of money, money like tycoons
and count christmas and birthdays like
cuckoos

fruit that will be
a big swag
too soon, and too long.

you
I'll not feel with my hands your unseen kicking
I'll not have your heart-breaking glance
or your eyelashes laid on your cheek
your arms thrown back
as you fall back asleep
in your indolence of milk
because you are a soul of trust
in your mother

because you are heartless and trustful, best beloved
and I'll not trust it would be better
I'll not be mrs. troll face
do this, do that, yelling,
with a thing, gnawing,
at my vitals for a decade again.

118

little daughter of the gulf,
you're deeper in than ovaries or womb
you
clumsy I am with you
your open eyes wander all night,
I take you for flesh of mine.

The Bath

this dark of which I am the face
this cave beach my canoe finger explores
stretched and ribbed like shipspars

or this cavemouth of water or blood
swamped

drifting anemones out
from my womb to sea
the lost fronds of a cradle unwound

a gentle loss
my finger winds a tiny curl of my leaving

— soft head
birthing myself in bathwater —

No Room in the Ark

Clever, weren't you, getting
paired off in time,
sandy-nosed or spotted or blue-bummed,
there you are now with nothing
to do
but chew cud and wait
till the water goes down.
But, because I'm single,
having wanted nobody in particular
blind to all the mad mating

the urgency of which passed utterly
over my head
as the water will now do shortly,
you wouldn't have me; Noah said
'no' firmly
and pushed me off with an oar.

Through a loudhailer he crossly explains
as I keep bobbing along side,
that it's marrieds only
— nobody told me that —
that they're packed out with loving couples,
camel, eagle, and swan, elephant
and blowfly, ape and worm
all in satisfactory conjugal state,
just as he and Mrs. Noah,
the whole in beautiful shipshape breeding order,
not a gnat going spare
en route for Arrarat.

He shouts he would be grateful if I
drown quickly please. I
am upsetting the more sensitive monkeys
and wasting supplies,
(they keep throwing me bananas
to keep up my morale.)

Goodbye, monkeys
here I sink
in the kind waste of your wake,
my shroud a water-logged banana-skin.
I am settling down,
Noah,
after all.

poem

you unwrap,
you unsquint your eyes cautiously
I am sorry; I see I
acted like some sort of doctor,
cruel to be kind, kind but firm etc

I dragged you out backwards,
clenched your barely known intelligence
before anything could be known
really; moulded you tartly
                    like a cook
with a large family to turn out for
(meat and two veg)
or a potter: more cups, they break,
                    trays of
identical beakers —

you would have come out in your own time

my despair might have stopped it,
we can't be certain
at least you exist,
half-done, dwarfed, off shape
meagre, a thin subsidized
at least you exist

I wrap you up in the most exalted
                    trimmings,
one must guard you

I was so hungry and thirsty for you

Medea

Medea, mother of witches
drawn by dragons in your getaway car
you got the rough edge of the world

princess of the high I.Q.
with ointments to stop bulls
and rip off fleeces
but stuck in smalltown Colchis

so you married to leave home
and sailed off with large Jason
you mixed tongues on the hard deck while the others rowed
and the sacred oak said, don't take her
she'll go bad

Medea mother of witches
you are the dark woman who presses on the door
and your head turns into a continuous scream
for not being let in
you're not the last to kill sons
and die in smoke
for not being let in

well, witch, in your fury
your teeth are stone-capped
your hair is sewn on
your breasts are tidy iron
my Medea, stop digging stones
smart dragons forget heroes

smart dragons who want the robbed jewel
whistle it back under their ermine breath

the long haired woman

burning out my throat
with the mildest cigarettes
listening from woman to woman
from house to pub to flat to cafe to house
    on the phone
to the next woman
with her blue eyes
and her thin breasts that I want to
    talk to as well
and her print-inked fingers
who reminds me of her own poem
of the woman with long hair met on a street
    (her hair floats, though in our backwaters)
and listening, and doing what I think's
    called gossiping
but it's not like that to me
more of a race: like a racehorse
where I pull back and let go, pull back
    and let go
and we racehorses all run together
headed into the wind
a great fatigue
but not mildewing and rotting and watching

To J

you, child
stop battering on the ceaseless door
that woman no longer exists
she exists not, d'you hear
therefore it cannot open
therefore it exists not, d'you hear
therefore spit on shadows
that spat on you
the worm that strangles your tongue
exists not
the worm in your piped guts
playing worn-out stops
exists not
round its white bled stem
where indeed there was a blood-letting
now you breathe, and your flesh is healthy
with cells you have fed and nursed
and cared for, seen strong
over hard years
these exist, your paths
these

I want you not to be deflected
 while mourning the past

KATHARYN ROSA GABRIELLA (Ph.D.)

*Born 4 September 1943, has been writing since a child. Lectured in English
Literature at several universities. Has written and published nearly 100 poems in
England as well as critical books and works on Blake. Since an adolescent, has
often done political organising, towards a radical (i.e., to source and revolutionar
revolutionary) human form of social life and realised freedom. I am a baptised,
confirmed, and communicant member of the Church of England. Years ago I
legally changed my old (last) name to be my own as my choice then became and
is, partly from feminist principles and most for spiritual considerations, so that
I am identified according to my loves, desires, and creations. Most of my life is
in my writings.*

D & C: Lar Mer-Maid Exploration
(for Robert Hunt, M.D., 20.IV.78)

Like a Hovercraft, floating between the channel, anti-gravid,
I am tipped, speculum separated, bottom
up, readied for the annual taking off and out
of the meager, proliferative endometrium.
Anchored in place with a metal tenaculum, like a two-
armed octopus, the cervix is twice injected with local

anesthesia — to fuel and numb the os for concentric waves
of dilations. We wait before ascent, like selective travellers.
The aspirator is unshored and connected to the water-
logged tubing. Then you insert, thro' the portal
cervix, the flexible cannula, and the suction
motor begins to vacuum out the ebbed contents
of my 'jetswoomb'. You navigate around
the liquid lining and draw out the salty nutrients
preserving this retroverted, sunken treasure;   ·
you aspirate a second round, not to miss
any retroflexive riches. The collected endometrial
lining is cultured, for microscopic
analysis, like a pearl, as thoroughly as sand
washed under the cytologic ocean.
We have avoided the hyperplastic
cancerous leviathan. We have gone
beyond the narrow straights of progeny. We are voyaging
across the red waters by aspiration
to discover blood-bearing auto-generation.

Exploitation de l'Oublie (27.IV.76)

Polite but strangers the first
time we hurried to a distant
bed, tourist-class, we now exchange
undressed stories, incursions
into private parts of our past
lives, like the scars
we have
to show
(unfaded)
we are mortal and have lived.
(Such tissues do not turn to fat
indifference.) Each, partly, political
prisoners, tho' admittedly loose,
like broken bones, in a minimum security
institution, we are forced
to struggle against whatever concrete
abstract systemmes turn us into public wounds
no court or currency can hide
away, or heal.

(I am not a foreign
country to be run
over, or occupied.
Politics are flesh.)

It's false to pretend
we mean anything special
to each other now, as if one limb
or organ were as good
as another. It's obscene
naturally to forget,
not to re-member the others
(whose names we do not know),
whose voices are screaming
(but we cannot hear),
whose bodies are being torn,
torn apart
(without description)
while we talk, lying
embedded in that deep silence
of unfinished scarring,
flagrant, but not yet seen.

One does not feel
the pain, however familiar,
of another: yet try to imagine
such constant breaking
open to live.

An Item from the BBC News (7 May 1973)

Women get paid one third less
in pension funds, since
they retire earlier
and they live more years
than men: as if the poorer
women get, the longer
and stronger women live.

KATH FRASER

Born 23rd April 1947 in London. I've spent all but 5½ years of my life around London, where my struggles were formulated — the fight for personal freedom and choice, which has naturally led to gradual affirmation of my identity as a lesbian feminist. Once a clinical psychologist, sometimes traveller, now a gardener, and still with dreams of taking myself seriously as a writer and sculptor. The imperative nature of my need for other women has finally broken through years of puritanism and liberalism.

Your eyes burn icy
and words spurt from your mind —
weapons you make to survive.
Your passion is such that you reach me even over the vast distance.
I think I am forgetting how to shout that far,
I only whisper,
I die rather than scream.
Soft smiles and sad eyes rather than
lusty bellows.
And I could
I could devastate the tower with my noise
and I don't.
Like the others I won't take the risk of my power,
I won't take my power
I choke and whisper dying words on swallowed rage.

They told me insanity came from fighting *against* being crazy —
but you are living out a craziness
and some call you mad.
Well, what is that?
It is hard to take the force,
absorb the blows.
So many of us women pretend such fragility.

SONG (October 1969)

I love you, Mrs. Acorn. Would your husband mind
if I kissed you under the autumn sun,
if my brown-leaf guilty passion made you blind
to his manly charms and fun?

I want you, Mrs. Acorn. Do you think you'll come
to see my tangled, windswept desires,
and visit me in my everchanging house of some
vision of winter's fires?

I am serious Mrs. Acorn, do you hear?
Forget your family and other ties,
Come with me to where there is no fear,
where we'll find summer butterflies.

I am serious Mrs. Acorn, are you deaf?

KATHLEEN MCKAY

Born 1953, went to comprehensive school in Kirkley near Liverpool. Went to Queen's University Belfast where scraped through Russian degree and edited the fortnightly student newspaper. Tried to start a poetry magazine in Belfast but it never got off the ground. Came to London 1975 to work as a volunteer in a kind of law centre. Have worked in a publishers and for solicitors. Had a son February 1978. While pregnant, started writing again. Interested in poetry as power. Fascinated by words and language and eventually would like to do more experimental work but, for a long time, think it will be hard graft learning how to write a simple descriptive poem.

Memories

'She 'ad to get married, yer know'
The memory came back to me as I sat on the bus back from the clinic
'She 'ad to, yer know'. 'She was five months gone
White wedding indeed — the bloody 'ippocrites'.
They would stand on street corners and discuss it —
the latest scandal, the latest pregnancy.
They all looked the same — mostly scrawny,
with a scarf round their heads, a fag out their mouth,
their legs blue and nobbled, shopping bags on hip.
I thought about what they said about me

'College girl' 'dead clever'.
'My daughters at university', my mother would say
proudly to the pub at large
whenever I went back.
And now three years out of college
and here I was, on the way back
the test had been positive
— I was one of those who in the past would have
''ad to get married'
I didn't have to now
just decide what to do.

To Phil (if he wakes up)

Anger
Anger drove me to it
I killed him at last
One night when we were alone in the house
And the stage was set for sex
And romance
and he fell asleep,
smelling of creosote and beer.
So I killed him. It was simple really
with a knife I had from the Guides
It was sharp and strong
So I found his heart and looked at him, sleeping and unaware
he'd always said he wanted to die in his sleep
the irony was good
I smiled at him once and the knife slid in, meeting resistance of flesh at first
and then something that felt like the gristle under my butchers knife in the
                                                                        kitchen
He looked up once before he died
And his eyes had that wide open, slightly surprised look of just before he came
and his tongue hung out like it always did
and then his body twitched and he died.

KAY STIRLING

Three years ago I stopped teaching; purchased a backpack; and flew from Australia to Thailand with my lover; because that was what HE wanted to do.

In Bangkok I bought a "Venus Composition Book" — complete with armless logo and 280 blue-lined pages. For nine months that's how they remained.

But, in London, in mid '76 I went to my first Women's Liberation conference, and discovered the Women's Arts Alliance. A year of informal sharing in the writing workshop contributed to a growing self confidence, and in '78 I started going to the poetry workshop.

More recently, my mouth of rebellion and protest is learning a new shape — the big round sounds of love. Working, living and loving with women has given this to me.

human nature

sex is a three letter word
word is a four letter word

the eskimoes had a word for it
— laughing —

but then that was a word
used by the men

out of generosity
they offered
their guests
a laugh with
their wife

the wives
always laughed
out of generosity

laughing
we say
fuck that

verse and voice

when i was sixteen
i had a long way to go

in the beginning
there was a honda step-thru
baby blue, a pillion for me
just the two of us
trundling on down
the back street and round the block
singing:

"Goin' up the country
Got to get away . . ."

you finished the song
and my tears flowed down to the yarra
where i went aboard

your pleasure cruiser and
sunned the deck
till the weather broke;
you put me on a life raft
i was carried out to sea

"How does it feel
to be on your own

with no direction home
a complete unknown?"

after forty days and forty nights
i became a white dove and dropped
glad tidings on the bridge of

your becalmed deck;
it was plain sailing for a month of sundays,
you in your oil skin, hard at the helm,
distributing fishes;
i was left holding the halyard.
we circumnavigated
your desert island, again and again
till we foundered

"Help! I need somebody's
help, not just anybody's"

a dashing silver sputnik came down from the skies,
announced:

"I am the Real Thing"

and rescued me.
i took advantage of the ride;
when we neared the mainland
i traded in my pink parka for a silk
parachute, put my feet inside
a pair of fur-lined flying boots
and jumped

i was high and dry

for six days i wandered the groove
with my diamond soles
and on the seventh
gave birth
to a miracle

she and i
have been firm friends
for years
in spite of the difference
in our ages, the relative size of our feet;

her eyes are blue where mine are green
and when they come together
there is recognition and
singing

"Wild plants are invaluable during times of famine or crisis,
precisely because they are wild. They are always there.
Waiting for their moment . . ."

Wild Rose

Dear Rosa,
        In '43
        500 tons of your rose-hips
        were used for Nation's Syrup.
        Collected from the hedgerows and woods
        you were found
        rich in vitamin 'C'
        equivalent to 25 million oranges.
        But you were estimated
        before then:

        In A.D.
        they sought your delicate unworldly scent,
        withstood your prickles, and
        pressed your blossoms
        into strings of beads;
        intended for the subdued fingers
        of other ladies-in-waiting.
        These Brides of Christ
        in counting
        contributed to your rape.

        In B.C.
        the Romans underestimated you;
        adorned their tables with your
        sweet pink petals, and
        dropped you from the ceiling.
        You had multiplied so successfully
        the guests were suffocated.

But then
they perfected you
in The Garden.
Or, so they thought.
But

Dear Rose,
You recognized
Your common status
just in time.
They tasted you
too much;
made you
ate you
You rose-honey
You rose-petal-jelly
You Turkish Delight.

"There is no nectar in the flowers of the wild roses, but they produce
abundant pollen, and either cross or self-pollination results."

LESLEY SAUNDERS

I was born in 1946 and my first child, Leon, a few months ago. I have been writing poetry for ten years; now I'm working on a book about women's experiences in childbirth. I also want to do a book soon of translations from the ancient Greek women poets — they are sadly invisible in the usual anthologies and I feel their poetry is another part of our past to be reclaimed: they need re-voicing through a woman. I would like to see poetry be again the powerful public thing it once was: I believe the poetry of women could accomplish this.

Voices [excerpt from a group of four poems]

First Voice:

I am a woman
of thirty years
proud with flesh
breasts and glistening belly distended
and from them my nipples and the navel-knot
jut startlingly out
for these months the three targets

of my bloodstream
huge they seem
gorging the creature that is not me
it is my body's bidding,
no escape

stepping out into the world
it is I who am inescapable
planted in life
pushing out sprouts
to crack the concrete
in our streets

Second Voice:

I am an old woman
the flesh on my forearms
is thinner and dry
and my breasts and womb are empty
whatever sons or daughters
I have had
have outgrown me.

I remember
my past was peopled once —
mother, father, lovers, friends,
a generation, a nation

now I am free to be alone
to rework the years
with the work of these barer days.
You want something from me.
What is it you want to hear?
Whatever I tell you,
you will go away impatient or sentimental.
No, I have left myself too much to do
in this surprising age
between fertility and death
I have a long way to go, and my own.
Leave me.

Third Voice:

My dark wet eyes
are sticky
and creased against
the glare
blood and mucus cover me
I cannot make words
my mouth
can only cry and suck
the long
naked
cleft
the fleshy folds and crests
between my restless thighs
speak
all
I am

.   I am the struggle to be born

Eleanor

The storm breaks
it is raining

on the wet dark soil
in the dark afternoon
a leaf rides
and rejoices
returning its flame
to the flow
of the earth

down down and down
the rain plunges and flows
in the black gleaming earth
too deep to follow

black water
leaps up through tunnels
and a salt dark flame
streams downwards

I celebrate the black riches
but
I do not understand them

you are the darkly-gleaming

'Klytemnestra'

At the turn of day I, Elektra,
with sandals and blown hair
— sibyl priestess sprite bitch —
walked, without my father,
out to where the mud flats frayed
into talking reeds
I follow my mother
Mother

that are no mother to me
but a childwoman
an aging infant
She is talking
she is always talking
(anything I don't say
will be taken down and used in evidence against me)
shut up shut up SHUT UP
trespassers on this brain
on this windswept dark terrain
will be executed
There is no room
in her tucked-up, tarted-up world
for hate or the mad howl:
nor any room for love and sacred song
Still we walk
I drive silence between us like an iron wedge
and the wilderness is surrounding us
leaden mist obliterating the sun
we stop where the water encroaches
and we know we shall silently fight to a death.

Winter, surreptitiously, rises from the earth
in the premature twilight, rises
to fill sky and mind
shutting out light till there are no shadows
locking it away in roots and withered wood
for a later time
but now   endless bleakness
I reel
the wind blows spaces through me
and the winter blots me out
— all is ash-greyness and wind-whispers
furrowing dry reeds and floodwater
I am possessed
but there are no prophecies or incantations.

At last it is time
Look round to face her
stare into her eyes, compel and receive the sign
endure the unforgivable recognition.

No!
She's gone
she has turned back
We have reached a truce
Not a peace —

truly, not a peace
for it is with myself I have fought
stared at myself with guilty eyes
raised my hand against my own head
I have wrestled with the whining child
who is stronger than a thousand men
the vengeful Child-Mother
who hunts and traps and possesses

and I am brotherless

Flesh of my flesh
our hearts beat together
and blood was exchanged
when I lay in your womb under your ribs
It is the rhythm that makes us walk together
here on no man's land at twilight
in the first hour of winter.

This winter will pass
but not until the victim land
is laid low and waste:
we must pace out the whole space
from heaven to hell before we arise.

I drink my bile
swallow it
down right to its source
while I watch her walking away
and though the taste is in my mouth
I have not choked to death

Mud and shingle swirl into darkness
as we reach the beach where we started,
stepping in unison
holding out hands for support on the stones

this truce may last a while longer.

Hermana-Madre

Mother
(not mine but Iruma's)
let me not forget
how we held each other
and I buried my face in your neck

I have dreamed
of this
holding and being held
in the warm circle
of another woman's body
the rounds of her (your) breasts
that can nourish an infant
the circle
of your (her) belly
that is a seat of comfort
the quilt of smell
and the net of hair
that filled my nostrils
and sealed me in
(from myself):
then we broke surface
the freshness of my tears
on your fingertips
and smiles in our faces

you gave me comfort
that I cannot give myself

I hold my child
close up to my cheek
nuzzle him
touch his face with fingertips
to catch some reflected comfort back

But I cannot be mother
to myself
The fire in the hearth
the potent earth-magic
the forbidden ancient word, beginning with M
(I dreamed these too)
— they might overwhelm me.
I need a flesh and blood woman

to hold me and show me
since my own mother has forgotten how
(but she is also the witch beneath my other skin
only hatred runs in her cold veins
and she grits her teeth in silent hatred
hatred lies behind her eyes) — deliver me!

I dreamed
my son
was still attached to me
by a great placenta
that I carried round:
and therefore I was forbidden
to enter the sea.

A mother's dream.

And his head
with the fine skull
and mauve veins threading
so close under the taut glowing membrane
of his skin —
how can this he
have come from me?
His gums pull the milk out of my long teats.
I am incomprehensible to myself
Shall I ever come to again?

Iruma's mother
I love you
For a while, I opened my eyes
into yours

I bury myself
in you
in my thoughts
and come up smiling.

LILIAN MOHIN

*Born in Kent, 1938, daughter of Jewish refugees. Grew up in small town
America, went to college, married, had two children. Returned to England
1970 and became part of the Women's Liberation Movement. Became angry,
active, a lesbian, divorced, a poet, a printer, awake: all these made possible by
the strength, love, criticism, clarity, gynergy I have met in consciousness raising
groups, among radical feminists, in a women's writers group.*

*As a member of Onlywomen Press I intend to find/encourage and print feminist
writing because I believe in the revolutionary power of words.*

sleep/power

I

you used to say you couldn't
sleep first or after I woke.

now you say
I'm the only one
you can close your eyes
turn your back on.

I always fell asleep first.
I was tired and I trusted me

if not you.
That's what I thought.

Now I watch you sleeping
(on those occasions
when we sleep near enough).
Have I learned
or unlearned something?

II

who falls asleep first
is about power

this time I slept first
but it was close

a race?

have we been
reading/writing the same poem

or doesn't it matter anymore?

III

back to back
or head to breast
we sleep well together
when we sleep,
well,
together

but sleep is rare
and I gobble it first

our fights unfocus
everything
starting with my eyes

in this game
the fact that you remain conscious
is supposed to mean I'm winning
it tastes of chalk
not losing
loss

144

This dream recurs (and is not obscure)

I seem to have two babies
both dead.
One is a girl of about two.
I don't know when she died.
She's been lying there for some time.
The other is a very tiny boy
perhaps three inches long.
He is kept in a small white cardboard box.
I had forgotten
to look in the box
for a long time, so he is somewhat shriveled.
I am concerned about papers, the authorities, death certificates.
A very young policeman comes to deal with the death
of the boy in the box.
I say it is a 'cot death' and/or "you can see how tiny he's always been."
Soon he is replaced by a policewoman.
It is necessary to cry.
They must not know I feel nothing.
She shows me some poetry. It is a test.
Reading, writing, or crying about poems gives me certain credit.
I look for some poems I have written to show her.
I cannot find anything appropriate.
The best ones are lost. She doesn't seem to notice.
I am concerned about whether to report
both deaths at once or to wait and then
report the girl's death. It is hard to work out
which will get me into more trouble.
Someone else's small round baby cuddles up to me.
It wears a white all-in-one suit made of towelling.
I hug it and pretend
to cry. My side feels good where the cuddling happens — nothing else.
I have to pretend to be distraught.
But I want to read an article in the Sunday paper (with pictures)
about how the print industry differs from country to country.
Something bad is going on.
It seems to thicken the air I have to breathe
and make it smell and taste of metal or plastic.
Those babies go on being dead.
Sudden fruit juice wouldn't help,
I know.
And anyway I would forget to water them tomorrow.
It is uncomfortable.

Radical Feminist Poem

in the kitchen she pivots
on one foot, the dance of
one hand opening
the door, depositing the eggshell where
she doesn't have to look
certain of foot and hand
rhythm, spinning, eye upon
the frying pan.

and the mountain goat
does she make of daring
habit?

Dear Daughter

we are not polite to each other
that's the way to tell
we are not
strangers

or by our mouths which
chant/refrain/resent
the safety hymn

or by the slow traditional
reflections
drip of the lost unquestionables
treading me now, alone.
summer fruit, your first flesh
hot solidity of skull and knee and glance
hair sweated to head in
such ferocious sleep night after night
in the eons before your years could be
proudly written in two numbers

all the known embarrassments and trusts
thin hairs of memories
I'm not sure are mine.
Is it true?
Did we love each other like that?
What do you know?

⊠   Too late for ignorance
long past peace
I can no longer reflect upon
my reflection;
all the mirrors are fractured,
no one I know looks back at me.

⊠   we come together, having chosen
to come

trust and distrust

six women sit around a table, breakfast over,
talking, yellow light on wary eyes,
eyes holding, letting go, holding,
a firm palm on one
sharp shoulder blade

we come together, having chosen
to come

The O.E.D. says trust is 'to do some action
with expectation of safety, or without
fear of the consequences'

safety isn't a realistic possibility
most of our consequences hurt

having chosen,
it is necessary to come together

not faith, but the slow swelling
of what we need; trust
wrung from our distrust
drop by globule
spoonfuls, speech, touch, cupfuls
a sea, our own tides.

LIZ TROTT

An afterthought, a post-war baby (30th April 1945), a foreigner both to my parents (Swiss/French/American) and the English people I've lived among, I grew chameleon skills to fit all the bills, and got married fast to see if that would fit. It was a very straight jacket. Finding the women's movement in 1972 met some needs and raised more and more questions. After shedding quite a few skins, sometimes uncomfortably, I feel good about the one I'm making now, with the help of a lot of women, and my three children. Continuing passions and hopes concern women, making gardens, language in general and Russian in particular.

CHILDLIFE

My daughter has put a red satin bow
on the black telephone   and I am happy.

She is in her room, privately counting
doll's furniture, necklaces, and pinups,
and   I am happy.

Even asleep, half in, half out of the
duvet, she seems to me contained in
herself, cheeky, dignified and sure
of me, because I am happy.

Not only that, she is already a woman
of our world, and of that one outside,
and gives me wise answers to grave
questions, tells me not to worry, so
of course I'm   happy.

She is twelve, I am thirty two,
and I'm waiting for the pay-off
yes, of course, but, meanwhile
you got it now? I'm happy.

PUB REFLECTIONS

The heavy, jealous eyes of the excluded
surround me, though carefully veiled,
or disguised as rich, lecherous or sociable.
They show so clearly the writhing spirit
trapped there; I cannot breathe their pain
for long.

So I drop my gaze: but still around these
persons lingers an exhaled greed for warmth,
for some hint that they are needed by the
fortunate ones, whom they conceive only
with images of felicity.

Do they not yet know, so burnt are they?
that all ache, envy, burn, are damned
also in every pore as they? Fine false
promises were we all given in childhood,
that we would emerge from the tunnel
of infancy, grown, into a kingdom of delight,
free will, grass, sky and trees.

Whatever the process of this pain,
it reeks, and stings even a casual
wordy lover, looking on from a corner.
All she may do is look away, for pity
and terror, and quickly conceal whatever
it was flew around the room, under
another cigarette, another beer.
Perhaps, in the end, she learns never
to raise her eyes from the newspaper.

�֍ Velvet you were for me
my love sunshine
glass thunder cruel too
a river, hailstones

let me be
a tree blowing
hawthorn, ruby fruit.

when upright
rooted I shall be
my own mistress
no longings too great
to be borne in flowers
no joy too strong
uprooting me from boulders.

no need of comfort
but sun and wind
rivers still flood
at thought of you
new branches waver.

✖ Oh I do like to be beside
the sea side
I do like to be
beside the sea
I do like to hit the nail on the head.
I like it that
when the wind blows
the cradle will rock
when the bough breaks
it will fall.
I do like long bumpy roads.
Yes I am
            greedy
yes
I do
      like women
and I do like women to be greedy.
Sometimes none of it fits
but still I do like to
be beside the sea.

150

LORNA CARMICHAEL

is a Scottish lesbian feminist. She is 24. She grew upon the island of Mull but is presently living in Edinburgh where she is involved with sister musicians in an attempt to establish a women's band. We'll get there!

Woman in Torosay

between the gates
and the water garden
along in Statue Walk
moss higher than ankle level
creeping between the fingers
blinding the stone still sight
then suddenly seeing her
an orange shirt bright
a hole on the right hand side
of an old woollen jumper

surprise simple pleasure
then off to crouch on lions
the common ground of childhood
it was then i caught the lines
with paint dribbling down

always that bit older
than i remember
a few more scars
a few more cracks of laughter
there are expressionless skins
but not this where the neck
pulls and tugs the flesh
sharply over the bone
and the hair flipped back
when she turned in the wind

too soon time
and previous well made plans
dispel sweet sounds
of voices and the fountain running
she jokes of seeing me alone
there is existence beyond the hill
stretch out and feel the rain
life is merely the passing of time
a little more or less
i touch her arm
turning to the eucalyptus
a forest leaning seaward to die

drawings sue madden
edinburgh festival 1976

two boys at the exhibition

so this is art
they giggle
pulling each
at the other's arm
they're not impressed
by lines and tones
of delicacy or depth
for them the bold reality
of process and blue
a wild fascination
for the yellow stream
from her leg
laughing warily
they touch the source
and trace the line

wandering

through the city
wondering sometimes
where you might be
just curious

through my head
puzzling
why you are there
guilty sometimes
when you are

through your arms   through your arms
feeling warm   losing hold
feeling strong   losing touch
swimming   drowning
with your darting tongue   in your distance

through the night
alone now
no fears about caring
too much for you
no reason
just thought

Kelly's Cavern

sitting with our sisters in this pub
and your arm rests light on my shoulder
talking laughing sharing

we are the only women in this pub
men playing billiards and other games
with thoughts of never losing
while our strength is a growing volcano
and i taste their fear in my pint

someone comes over clearing glasses
my hand is easy between your thighs
i think about moving out to safer limbs
as you talk to dykes about jackets

you might have bought
your thighs tighten
and our personal
is political

unlike the glasses
we cannot be washed out

⬧   trapped in this shell
                               and you woman kiss my lips
                               bring the inside out
                               taste the blood
                               leave me painless
                               without form

        sometimes
        when she leaves my room
        a small pain
        eats into my head
        crying laughing silent
        a space to be filled or not
        she comes in like a river
        and leaves like the wind

                               where now
                               tunnelling through my veins
                               no direction
                               a lightning flash
                               smother the waves
                               build dams
                               around the spring

LORNA MITCHELL

I am a member of a recently formed Feminist writers' group in Scotland. We are hoping to begin producing a magazine next year. We have come up against the problem of how Feminists approach critical judgement of poetry. I think there are some objective standards which we should try to articulate but they are limited. But within these limitations — judgements are highly subjective and Feminists should always be aware of this and avoid replacing the old male elitism with the same thing in feminist guise.

Free Association To The Tune Of 'Women In Ireland'

I write coherent sentences even in poems. I always look back on what
I have written to see what I want to say.
"How can I know what I think till I see what I say?" said Alice.
(The women of Ireland keen like the sound of the wind, on the hills,
whirling mist, turntable.)
Sarah wears a scarf round her neck. She dresses carefully. Alfred says
she is mature.
Alice saw the white rabbit, with a scarf round her neck. She was in a
hurry. She was too busy to talk. She ran by like a film reel again and
again and again.
"I'm late, I'm late, for a very important date"

But is she mature? I have lost my sense of time.
(Women of Ireland I am lost in a whirling mist,
I am blindfolded by the sound of your keening)

There are so many quotations churning in my brain. Is it other people's
experience or my own? What have I experienced? I understand infinity. I
am terrified of death. I am strung out on all points between. I look back
on what I have been to see what I am. I have been here before.
"I am half-sick of shadows" said the Lady of Shalot, locked in unreality.
She wanted to be Lancelot. But when she broke outside, the curse was put
upon her and she died.

I didn't see the children today. I saw myself as a child. I saw myself
as my parents.
(Flute in the sky rainbow playing dying)
Dying: for you dark church on sunday. For us breakfast, black pudding,
potato scones, bacon, eggs, tomatoes.
Alfred talks about the book he reads. He is going to university soon.
I am afraid he will get caught up in intellectual crossword puzzles.
We had cross words with Alfred yesterday. We cornered him for saying Pam
and Sarah were more mature than us. "I am cross" says Pam. She folds her
arms in front of her and looks down at us from a greater height. But is
she more mature?
When she spoke the small child hid under the desk lid the hollow swirling mist
below the breast
"Rock of Ages cleft for me"
"These children need security"
Said the teacher
And firmly placed them in their niche
In the Rock of Ages
At the top the academic labyrinth
Where the darkness swallows you and you turn into a flapping scrawny bat
Endlessly emptily flapping from corridor to corridor. Total absorption
is a trap. My soul flies out of it.
My soul is with the women of Ireland.
My soul is not trapped in music sex or politics
I am painting my own picture of my life with any materials that seem to
have creative use. Some of these might be quotations.
In the past I made a religion of literature. I no longer have that faith.
I am my own religion and I am a sinner. I fall from my own grace when
I dont believe I'm good.

I'm not secure in my belief in myself.
Sarah wears a scarf as part of her security of self image.
The hanged man wears a rope round his neck.
"I have experienced death" she said.

"Death" said Wittgenstein "is not an experience that is lived through"
The edge of death is like a river bank. We are lost in the jungle or hide
in our hut in the clearing. If we keep the river in sight, we can choose
the straight route and ignore the tangled bushes. That are not important.
(The strings are lengthening tightening spindleing —)
"Strings and sealing wax" and "ships and shoes" and ships on the dark
river. Conrad sailed on a ship through the Congo jungle and experienced
the heart of darkness. Death power and Imperialism.
The imperialism of the mind. My father was a sailor. I identified with
him through Conrad. I was a sailor in my mind.
Men's experience or my own? I identified with male heroes in books.
Heroes in books. Heroines in real life. Two cultures: their's and my own.
My heroines: my sister Helen, her friend Janan her friend Elizabeth
My mother's friend Aunt May who died.
"She was very afraid of death" said my mother.
My mother without her false teeth in. Her sunken mouth. Death in the
wings.
My mother and me. We used to go to the theatre. We saw the dying Franz in
the 'Condemned of Altona' locked in his attic unreality. Wracked with
guilt for killing Jews. Pompously haranguing his oyster shells.
I held my mother's arm and we went home to tea:
                    black pudding, potato scones, bacon, eggs, tomatoes.
I thought "Someday I want to write a play like that"
It takes time to write a play about wasted time.
Do I want to use it up?
Spending time is wallowing in a pigsty
And wisdom is a pearl sometimes found there.
"Socrates" they said "was the wisest man on earth"
He said he knew nothing
"He didn't live through what I've lived through" says the middle aged
women in a play not yet written.

I still haven't written that play.
Have I wasted my time?
"Mothers and children, that's all there is" says an old lady in a New
York geriatric home.

Who are you mourning for Women of Ireland? Your children or yourselves?
My mother has spent much of her life living for others. Has she wasted
her time? Is she mature?
Mother we are both dying minute by minute. We have all the time there is
Will we be late for our own funeral?
                    or early?

LYNN ALDERSON

30 years old, feminist lesbian, works in bookshops, Sisterwrite at the moment.
I don't really think that what I write is poetry — not enough craft, awareness of
form and broadness of vision. I write to explore my personal mythology and
symbols, in response to strong emotions. It's part of the process of relating to
women and the essential "making conscious", the need to describe and share
which I think is crucial to ourselves as feminists.

You gave me
the dry solid stones of your words
dropping in the dark
where we lay.

Embedded in the flesh of my breasts
I wear them
with straight spine
and silver spear.
Sharp pointed star value
they cost us both
my dear.

⊠. Last night,
everything seemed possible
today
I cannot write this poem on lovemaking.
Notes.
your head on my belly
your breasts between my thighs
my legs cradle you
my fingers fit neatly into
your ears
closing off all sounds
save in the blood and the breath
"It sounds like"
I said
"in a shell"
you finished
-- the sea in a shell
you fit round me
I fit round you
your finger moves
from my clitoris,
slowly,
up
between the breasts
the neck
centering
splitting me
to the head --
the links I cannot make
for myself.

⊠ you leave the taste
bitter like cigarettes
on my lips and tongue.
I am tired of all
the perambulations,
mothers and babies,
wheeling round
in the sky
a flock of crows
all black in the distance --
it is a matter of indifference
whose toes curl around the branch.
Tonight I shall clean my teeth,
tomorrow
whose next?

Shetland poem

We have shared the wild winds
sand biting into our faces
cutting, howling through our bodies —
each step a struggle
each bend towards home
a victory
in the dancing singing madness
of the night gone black

Now I look for other companions,
(friend too soft and frail a word)
other women
who love the raging hurricane
and can bear a million tiny stings
and still,
bending seeing nothing,
go on . . .

Our days of battling storms are gone
and much bitterness
and ragged flesh remains,
in the welter of old lovers' hurts
I sometimes forget
that we actually made it home that night
and that you laughed
in its teeth —
as did I.

MARGARET de V. WILLS

Born Derbyshire 1926. Had literary and stage aspirations but became a nurse (it was wartime) in London. Married, had seven children, and travelled a lot, bewildered by eternally trying to cope. It all seemed personal and inevitable. I really woke up too late. Far worse — I can't see how other women can avert the final disaster. We seem to need some impossible, some Cosmic, Lysistrata.

Badger

the badger — squeezed in a vice
the maddest corset maker never dreamed of —
diameter to be precise —
three inches the steel trap's ring—
her burst belly — trailing dugs
dragged two miles through the woods
to find her young ....
                to weigh
alternatives — wonder if she could make it —
or to stay —
split sausage that she was —
a toothpaste tube stoppered
both ends, eviscerated as
a cycle wheel had clobbered it —
did not, I would presume —
occur to her — nor assume

an image on the retina
of whimpering lost faces
nosing for milk she leaks
as - - staining the grasses red
she stumbles — cleft
her way til she was dead

so far so good
and yet — no animal must plan
of when to hold — leave —
but a woman ....
is there some ganglion from lobe to loin
unfailingly connected in a lion,
a swan — in us left loose
to tie on our children
tight as an epileptic's jaw
his tongue on .... ?

'Some Women of Marrakesh'

Strange as the Star in the Major Arcana,
Strange as the Queens of the Looking Glass Lands,
Women of Marrakesh dance for each other,
Snaking silk hips to the beat of their hands.

Veiled from the street, to the tower unbidden,
Free from the mosque's mathematical prayer,
In cedarwood rooms, upon white flaking balconies
Marrakesh women meet, faces all bare.

Hidden by walls built by Sons of the Prophet,
Square walls confounding men's hard horny stare,
Circles are magicked by Marrakesh women
With swirling black brushes of gyrating hair.

Through caverns uncharted by husbands of Islam,
With passion escaping men's measuring rods,
As underground streams find a way to the rock face,
Marrakesh women keep tryst with the gods.

Gods who are tumbled by Marrakesh women,
Gods who are humbled, resist if they dare
The terrible torrent the Marrakesh Goddesses
Loose as the thundering water hits air . . .

Roses of Jericho, bloomed in a prison
In juices distilled in the long skirted trance,
Goddess of Rebirth, fronded from flesh dew,
Glimpsed through the Marrakesh women who dance.

Where will you go when your roots are all shattered,
How shall you grow when your garden is gone,
Starkened your stems and your petals all scattered,
Torn by the concrete and seared by the sun . . . ?

Footsore for centuries, bruise eyed from weeping,
Clutching the tat of the cloak she once wore,
Wrenching the lattice where daughters lie sleeping,
Banging on bolts with her knuckles beef raw,

Searching through shops, through the offices, factories,
Haggard from aeons pressganged on the game,
Rouging her cheeks in bordello poxed moon glass,
Crack throated Ceres is calling your name . . . .

Somewhere in shadow awaits dark Diana,
Fledging her fury and biding her chance,
Drawing a bead on the bonds of the Goddess
Grown by the Marrakesh women who dance.

Astarte in Green Shawl

Pepa   Lola   Concha
sitting on a chair
make up tawdry
clapping hands for
Pepa   Lola   Concha
shaping air for them

Now it's your turn. In the
spotlight Venus rises
in silk flounces
incense from forgotten ashtrays
prayers of thickened little men

You are in your own place
even the guitars can't reach you

where you are though dark heads
bend and fingers flail to frenzy
Seas and skirts are in your arms
and in your eyes an Ultimate

Soon   You'll   be
Pepa Lola Concha
sucking straws in backstage
wiping paint and sweat from back hair
walking mortal down a backstair
eating yellow rice
drinking yellow wine
dance for us tomorrow
dance again tomorrow
dance
dance
dance

Aradia
Aphrodite
my
Astarte in green shawl.

Emergency Ward New Year's Eve

once there was a night
when the man whose mother's face you have
and i   lay in a low wide bed
and in the after silence you were there too.

the night when you and i lay in the harsh light
guy fawkes night   rockets and bursting stars
in me   and then the cord pumping last blood into you
before they parted us with steel clamps and scissors
our hair was wet and we were weary and the bed was hard
you cried with shocked first breath outrage while
i cried and laughed and puked into the white bowl.

tonight i watch you in your high white bed
the ward light low
wet and black your hair upon the pillow
pain claws in your woman's belly

weary beyond sound
from your arm a tube snakes to a jar above your head
red wine in this light and the third litre
my hair wet and the chair hard and nineteen years of you
i look at the wine label
it says B positive
sweet christ we are both B positive
so this time we could use a plastic cord
and this time you could have it all girl
as a new year present
from mother   with love

IT

All myths die hard and won't lie down,
None more so than our very own;
The You and Me Together one.

For years we kept It live and well
On Compromise, Concession, Repression
In little bottles on the bathroom shelf.

We spiked Its nightcap . . . .
Tiptoed red eyed in the morning
Only to find It calling
For Its tea,
          and cancellation
Of the court decree
We had decided on . . . .

When the men come, if they ever come,
Wearing black socks,
They'll have to break Its bones
To get It in the box;

And even then, it's said
There are tales . . . . . .
                    of the
                         Undead.

MARGOT LIDSTONE SINHA

I am 25 and now live in Birmingham — having previously lived in Brighton and on Anglesey. I think feminist writing is the work of women who are questioning — or have questioned in the past — the assumptions of their society. It explores and presents alternative viewpoints and structures. One particular area in which this seems very important to me is literature for children, and this is what i'm trying to produce at the moment. I am also doing research into modern women's writing — including science fiction — and hope that this work will be useful to myself and other women in understanding our self-images and our position within a male culture and society.

A change of climate.

My mother lived
in temperate zones.
Warmth rose,
steamed and soaped;
a day baked waits
in vacant afternoons
for lives returning;
clothes piled pressed
and folded hours.
    Actions complete

a day, a week, only,
while repetition extends
to consumption of time.
    Debt written off,
no record of shames
subdued and guilt
garnished the joint on Sundays.

My mother multiplies in me whether I refuse or remember;
A child unable, I, to instruct or to profit.
For earth tilts now its axis,
tropic and pole extend across her familiar sureties.
Mother you are the fire and its food in me.
Shames flourish in a hot land,
guilt freezes well.

MARG YEO

I was born, in Canada, in 1946, and I'm a Cancer, which I think is fairly revealing about me. Till about three years ago, I was working on a Ph.D. in English and teaching at a Canadian university; then, luckily, it occurred to me that things academic weren't really for me, and I got out. The Canada Council stepped in at that point and gave me two writing fellowships, the second of which included a travel grant which brought me to London. Now I'm settled here, happy, living collectively, and working with a women's poetry workshop.

if we walk out

if we walk out at all
it is through poems

finally we condemn
nothing but fear,
though we are most
fearful: thus

we condemn ourselves,
such imperfection, such
humanity

we are not apart
from this world, we are
apportioned into it, never
weary with conjunction

never weary of speaking
it imperfectly, its own
imperfections rescue
us from too much fear

for loving whole

so it comes
sudden and
huge, the thick
filling pain swallowed
with knowing:

(watching her step down slowly
from the plane, eyes filling up
with tears like watermelons,
i ate unsaid love, ate
pride, pain) i remember
everything, salt taste of quarrels
and tears, body i occupied
while this flesh grew
whole, came to seem
separate

truth is, i am this woman's
other arm, face, flesh: sudden and
whole and huge i carry my
mother in me, occupy the bare
spare generation between us
with this quick, labouring love

faith   the vivisector

mandy introduces: all
                                        to
'this is my friend   gether
faith'   too
        it knocks me   painful, pocked, the
over, faith   surface of the world,
for a friend; i am   show
impressed with the sheer   this, not washing the bare bone
solidity of it   edges sentimental,
              she   pastel, and
drinks, rolls an immense   see, no one wants to
joint, takes her shoes   glimpse the naked
off, discourses over   wrenched body, opened for
dinner on the libidinous   truth to flow
follies of smoking
              pumps   it is always
up with supreme   too painful, opening flesh bare
confidence (what   to the bone, wrenching out agony
else?) every   in trees or the piercing
thing, including her   song grass keens as it
self, into which air can be   dies thru august
introduced by the furious
stamping of a foot on a rubber   too
accordion; she races small   painful, even for the

cars on an eccentric   vivisector, who opens her
track round the room (they   self as
shoot off or jam   well, eagerly, hoping she has
at the corners, but faith   this time torn
believes, plunges   out the
them back, and they rush round   heart of it
and round, un-
imaginably courageous)   and
                                        still
                  she collects her   keeping it
self (must   alive
leave) and is all at
once gone

leaving an all
too palpable space where
faith sat, eating such
dangerous eclairs

the beast in us

again
quick belly
twisting revulsion at the
beast in us, clever
instincts for fuck and
fight, for blood
lush meat, teeth
tearing at any
flesh
      without the belly
rich warm
shape of the known
body under hand
          shaping
of a one
thing out of
two, the need most not
to devour, to
offer up a
hand, head, quick
torso, legs to wrap up
in whole

         the need to make
love, in
faith

MARY COGHILL

I was born in 1952 and then again in 1976 when I discovered the Women's Movement. Words have always fascinated me but it is only recently that I've been able to say what I wanted with them; I always used to go blank when I tried to find out what was really important to me. I began to study pre-history with the Matriarchy Study Group and using this as a beginning from which to explore new identifications and moods I began to discard the receptivity and passivity women are always supposed to express. Now I can interpret those angry, cyclical, wandering, misty, fierce, calm, sharp, gentle, strong feelings and thoughts I have always had and no longer have to deny them. With these I can define my Self and, with the strength that the Women's Movement gives us, carry that definition of myself into furthering New Women's thought. This is what I try to say in my poetry.

GODDESS CREATION.

Creating a Goddess was too much work
For me to do it on my own.
Oh yes I knew the names of, Isis,
Diana, Rhea, Astarte, Ge,
And nearer to my own wan life
Cleo, Sheba, Jezebel, Helen.
But further, for didn't they die

Seem merely to be weak and mortal?
Just like a woman I thought then.
But those stories, how I loved them,
Read them, lingered, wondered, "Could I . . . ?"
Nothing answered, no reason why
And sadly, no cause, no end, no thought,
I forgot them saying, "It's just that
I am too stupid to understand."
I sighed while absorbing beauty
Spellbound I sought out trees and plants,
Felt soft turf, kind winds, and listened
To the sea waves break and birds singing,
Clung to hills and valleys, sweeping heights,
Soft womb like warmth and peace in hollows,
Ever quiet eternity, whole and growing.
Here I was at home and strangely rested
Never daring to stay for ever
Saying always, cold and heavy heart:
"As of Man I am thus lies my way."

But a woman never dies, gives up,
Of a woman born, and child bearing
She knows she's linked to all that's gone
To all that is and all that will be.
Silently, somehow and deeply wise
I waited my turn to come around,
And growing older, began to learn,
Be battle scarred, then hardened —
As I am so must I be, I will rejoice.

It's here a circle of shining faces
Rise to greet me, quite by the way
For them, but stunning and strange to me.
New knowledge of past times you showed me,
Here Goddess reigned, not God and gave
Earth verdant fruition not searing steel.

I'm laughing now, to know through flashes
Great caves of joy and warm pools of light,
The knowledge which spun sparkling past me.
First slow and afraid, then hungrily
I gathered such wanton presents to me
Whirling, then calmer, finally waiting
I can touch, choose, be delighted then take
All this new gladness, make it mine.

For now I know that these bright starred names
Echo all that previous calm and oneness,
No more an agony, misplaced sense
But a fulsome creation, Goddess given
In everything that be, and greatest,
In me embodied with all her signs.

No longer awkward I am gentle,
For where nature flows and ceaseless
Cycles run, aren't these the places where
I meld and blend, past feeling told me so.
So embrace the tree that rises sure
And royally to the sky and fold in
The greens and fruits of myriad things.
As She with branch and leaf, twined snake,
Round fruit, stone circle, queenly awe
Revealed herself, so I stand open,
Waiting, for this bounty is mine too.
With such a past behind me, I am;
This future for my asking, I can be,
Like these queens, great woman.

Vista in Whittington Park

She saw time rooted in an avenue of saplings;
She walked through her domain again for the first time;
In a hiatus caused by well planned habits
She saw life without her through a high window;
Through the distance she focussed on its stir within her.

What would you do, given a magnified pinpoint of sunlight?

She played notes simply, watched by waiting eyes of children:
She dug her own pass through time's own:
She put off unthought of emotions present to her:
She witnessed her feet unwittingly washed by a tide of words:
She put all her colours back into her crystal:
Then she unfolded her pictures; their colours catch the light.

Haven't you seen sun shining on wet sapling's leaves?

THIS IS THE MOMENT : THEN.

Release me; Daimons, I call you,
I would open wide my arms if I need:
I am gone, am not here, not now
Before my face becomes like the moon.

Breathe the haah, shut eyes, lean back,
clench hands, then open, relax,
the journey's done with this power settled in me;
If you blench, you are warned to remember —
I rest secure with my strength, just that.

And I speak to you from my calm centre,
I am a settled mound, cool with the cover of soft grass.
I am as strong and as gentle as the wind,
Timeless and passing as the plants grow,
Sturdy and humble as the great trees,
Young, bright, tender as the shoot,
Rich, sensuous, satiate as the fruit.
I am as ethereal as the daylight sky,
I am as close and enveloping as the dark night.
As the sun shines, I am life-giver and non-bodied,
As I am life I flow and bend with the moon strength.

I can hold you in my womb or stand beside you
Face, turn, hold or beckon, reflect or prove you.
If you hear these vibrant rhythms
You will catch my dance, fleet foot, light laugh,
My explosion of joy, all these, all in me.

I care with all these, have balance, wholeness,
I love.
Drawing from all this that I am around me, into me,
I am.

I know my mystery, as I stand here talking
You are the other that is also the other than me,
You are the part of me that is as much as I:
As I am, you are, and personally, I love you.

THE TIDE.

Well, so what have you been doing with your evening —
working?
Yes and I'm savouring the calm of the day's end
thinking,
the words and ideas rolling from the murmuring sea
flowing
and ebbing to an indeterminate end
the gaps
are that I never thought of fragrant breezes
a breath
of the air swirling as I went through a door
and that
I never think of others at all
always
I'm thinking of my own emotions and pains.
I pause
Can I correct this? What have I done today?
Meeting
the ladies this morning, I'm bored already.
"Go on"
I cannot and my pen drops with lassitude
interest
lies in other things, my confidence, my lover
and thus
thought's over, the beginning is a bad end
and now
the tide ebbs, cold wind blows over spent water,
to bed.

MARY MICHAELS

Born in 1946. She taught Art History for several years in England and in the United States, where she was also involved in producing a weekly radio programme about poetry and in feminist visual arts projects. (She has spent time in Spain and Mexico.) Her poetry has appeared in various magazines and anthologies (and she has published a booklet on feminist education entitled 'Learning to be there . . .'.) She now lives in London and works as a Librarian.

evening

the line is hung with harsh bright clothes
acrylic black, blue, yellow

down at the end
the woman from next door
is pinning up the last
a grey shirt

her face red-brown with the just-set sun
the green of her dress looking alive

a big moon is already high up
in the magenta sky

the folds of the mountains below
are losing their warmth and definition

odd
how the women put out their washing
late in the evening

as if it will ripen
in secret
like blackberries
with the dew

it must only get wetter
early and late

as the clothes hang
quietly losing their colour
like things thrown out
and forgotten

with the onset
of night

MARY WOODWARD

I'm 32, commonly regarded as an overeducated bad tempered frigid school-mistress. I like children, animals and people who write poetry.

well what do i want now now that i'm nearly thirty two:
a white house and my plants to grow, the laurel to do well
and the lavender to flourish and the camellia to flower and
inside all to be very cool and very quiet and there must be
music and books and at night there will be locks to be
locked and darkness to be kept outside where it belongs

and i want to be myself and to stop needing to think that
i'm the Witch of Atlas and for that to include the writing

and then to become what i began to be a long time ago   real
within words   though being a woman has made it very difficult
and my feelings have never been the instruments of truth that
my mind has. I want all this not just for myself but for

everyone: to be what they began to be when they were young and
all houses were white and quiet, and there was enough music

and the right words and things to be said and listened to.

heroine

her heart had been eaten by owls
and she had learnt to live without it

preferring somehow that odd freedom
to her old state in which there had

always been something to protect. Now
at last when she walked through the

trees at night she had become the
one who was really herself and they

the ones who rustled in vain in the
dark for the necessary lost for ever

answers .

 i begin to remember
what being cold's like

i pull decision round
me like my old fur
coat, walking through

the park. There should
be no need for all

this. See the geese
take to the cold water
with silent simplicity

i have done that before
and will again this winter

summer of 76, spent working in Barnet Hospital
but still going to a woman's group in Clapham

London, this late
Tuesday afternoon.
Mid August lying warm
children talking at the
other end of the carriage.

Simple familiar journeys
are like sleeping chances
for renewal. The day past

has been kissed by the
old and mad   with those
kisses I travel towards
the evening   and its
politics   mid August

the train slipping
through the London
names as the day moves

away

look at us old woman
my lucidity has been
dearly bought and
fiercely defended. In
this city in such a
summer did you laugh
and travel with the
children who haunt you
now losing even then
your direction
your clarity

yet your lunatic and
joyful sense of
sisterhood has coloured
the day gives this
late summer evening
more warmth

the little ghosts
of the children
I have never had

sit with me on trains
run before me
in the street

a subtle and sinister
mischief informs
their laughter

much as question marks
distort the clean
statement
they shift and undermine
the wholeness
of my undelivered state.

Because Virginia Woolf always goes into hardback first.

didn't have the money
to pay for it, the first
volume of your diary.

A woman remarking the
texture of cake at tea,

buying an apricot coloured
coat on her way home.

Lucidity week
after week,

and then the entries
stop for madness: fight
your way to 1918 and

skies and trees. Life
rewon, every detail to
be loved.

Being my own woman means
I stand in shops
to read all this.

⬙ simply this
that words not only
tell

but are part of
change   are

weapons to
strengthen a case

my words she thought
were once
emeralds   pearls
diamonds
my thoughts become
precise material
precious

now they are forceps
files   hammers

MICHELENE WANDOR

is a socialist and a feminist; she has been Poetry Editor and theatre critic for Time Out *magazine since 1971, and writes plays for theatre, radio and TV. She compiled* The Body Politic *(Stage 1) a collection of British women's liberation writings, together with Michele Roberts she edited* Cutlasses & Earrings, *an anthology of feminist poetry, and contributed to* Tales I Tell my Mother *(Journeyman Press), a collection of feminist short stories. She has two sons.*

London airport

gone in the air, the bird

on the plane, departure point
always a fine line between
too early and too late, waved goodbye before they
left, never get the moment quite right,
such a fine line between presence
and past, such a quick
move between now you see it, now
you don't, times and spaces back
where you come from the same (give or take
a change in air current or two)

the parts flow into reason's
corners and you can lay it all
out in order and still it
doesn't make a sense that
corresponds the mind's working
to the feeling

                     so they have (poets)
tried for centuries to find greater meaning
in the event than
momentary sadness; what are we to project?
'that all must go' (in death or international
travel; define the difference)
'that nothing stays in one place'
'that   change is life's rich source of
tragedy and happiness for God's sake'

such mechanisms are rusty; rasp as you listen
are no longer in accord with the event and its
history
        still holding onto the rift between what has
actually happened and the emptiness, let us reject
some of the old means and grope towards a
new accuracy:
            a domestic division means two children
move between two homes. The symmetry is fitful,
the feeling a protest at unnecessary pain.
The answer?

Make sure no more unions of this kind
(you know its name)
take place; build houses of many people
so no child need leave one home for another
and cross deserts on the way.
Make all houses big and make them homes,
Make all people lovers and parents, make one
word mean that. Make
unions of rivers so that no-one can tell
where one ends and another begins and
then stand at airports and wave goodbye and
smile into the tea; time and space are to
be welcomed and crossed, not feared

'how' is another poem

the occasional moment

sticking labels on squeaking
cooled down jamjars

sun strikes the glass outside
warming reminders of boiling
point

the labels conceal different parts
of the people inside
each jar

every one with its
date
for reference
neatly, above
a greaseproof circle
straining false scandals

what we have tried to make
is something new
something fresh
and sweet
something to be preserved

for a start, put them neatly
in rows on the shelf

at greater leisure
and possible risk
choose the first
to be tasted

Birth

I have a child
I have another child
I had the first one first
and the second one second.

But perhaps I over-simplify.

PIN MONEY

my mother pinned my wedding white
with a hundred silver pins
now each pin takes a message
from me to you:

pin money
pin money
pins the day together; makes the
                                difference
between no shoes and shoe leather
for us all

come look through my window
see my red, blue, pink and gold
soft tissues wrap your pleasure
snap your Christmas crackers
in here it's Christmas
every day of
of the year

I'm a home worker
a worker
who works
at home   for

pin money
pin money
pins the minutes to my fingers
pins my fingers to the table
to the floor

come buy your wedding dresses
stitch by flower
my fingers made them
hour by hour
once a lifetime for you
in here it's a wedding day
every day
of the year

pin money
pin money
pins the patches on my marriage
pins my marriage to the wall
over time

come buy my stuffed tigers
soft furry coats
soothe your babies to sleep
on their birthday
in here it's a birthday
every day
of the year

I'm a home worker
a worker
who works
at home   for   pin money
                                            pin money
                                            spreads my bread with pins and honey
                                            till I drop

June 1974

Hey, she said, write a poem she said
well, I said, no names, no places, no dates
no times, just a series of pronouns and
verbs and the odd adjective or two.
doesn't do
to expose me and my friends, my family, the
odd lover, the even odder never-lover
(well, we never got it together)

so we sat down together, cheek
to swing of hair and looked through books
and talked through each other and
wrote this poem together and typed it
out and listened quite quietly

while the others (ok, I'll come clean, the others
were women . . .) argued over it.
It doesn't like women, said one.
It doesn't like *some* women, we thought.
It is very anti-working class, said one:
It is anti-working class sexism, we thought.
(Remember, we conveyed through glances — remember
the time past the building sites at dusk
when they wouldn't let us past, we weren't
even dolled up . . .)

187

the grammar isn't right, said one.
Sometimes you want to explode syntax, we thought.
Why can't you say what you *mean* said one.
That's a jolting electric image, we thought.
Anyway, poetry is moribund, she said.
Moribund? We thought? Ever since Mr.
Marx got down to the British Museum
lots of people having been singing the
death-knell of capitalism; I mean,
it has to lie down before you can pronounce it
dead, we thought.

and we had a little wonder to ourselves
about them who dance like fury to Stones
raping words, to Rod Stewart piggery,
and allow the moribund bits of them
at their need for rhythm.

Naaa, I said, I don't want to write a poem.
I feel so — well, so sort of — well, exposed,
don't want my struggling content condemned because
it has to use a tired form till the old have
withered off the edge.
Keep myself to myself, I thought, drink
my coffee, do my work, smile and try
not to lose my temper or get upset
because nobody's got *time* (well, only the
odd lover and the kids) to look at my ol'
moribund feelings.

Hey, she said, you liar, you've
written a poem.

I'll be mother

got a cold? she tells me
your nose is running, she suggests,
you're tired
you're going to sleep, she says

she would not like me to be dead
because then she would have to grieve

she just wants me to be asleep
no trouble,
just breathing
so she feels she's done her duty

that way she won't remember
the blackout curtains
the ladder
the tacks
the jumping up and down
from the floor to the chair
from the chair to the table
from the table up the ladder
and the same in reverse
to make the stubborn foetus
dislodge in a cloud of unnecessary blood

abortions were rare and dangerous things in those days,
she says

I have a little cold
I shall have a little snooze
and then I'll wake up
so bloody there.

Some Male Poets

They write poems about
the softness of our skin
the curve and softness
in our eye
the declivity of our waist
as we recline

we are their peace, their consolation

they do not write of the rage
quivering

we snuggle perfection in
the ball of our foot
our hair weaves
glowing by lamplight
as we wait for the step
on the step

they have not written of
the power in

we approach divinity in
our life-source
we are earth-mother
yearned for
absent muse
shed a silent tear for
missed and loved

we are their comfort, their inspiration

sometimes we are regretted
when we behave
like a jealous woman
and loved for
our jealousy which
shows our devotion

they have not written of

and when we have begun to
speak of it, limping
coarsely, our eyes
red with sleepless pyramids

they have written of us as
whores, devouring Liliths

and never as

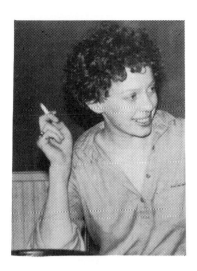

MICHÈLE ROBERTS

lives with three friends in west London and earns her living through office work.
She participated in the various women writers collectives which produced the
anthologies of poems Cutlasses and earrings *(Playbooks, 1976) and* Licking the
bed clean *(Teeth Imprints, 1978), and the collection of short stories* Tales I tell
my mother *(Journeyman Press, 1978). Her first novel,* A piece of the night, *was*
published in 1978 by The Women's Press. Besides working, she also enjoys
friendships, going dancing and walking, music, cooking, and looking at paintings.

to a man

you say
colour is clear
fields lie, little
tucked-up
beds of taut green silk
an orange car comes by
glossy as caramel, colts
kick up their smart white socks

I tell you
look again
brown is brighter than shorn curls
and bronze ditches
are deep with the purple of figs

the hedges' olive mouths
are stained with plums
those forests flush, that
beech-flame interrupts
the willows' silver-grey

only your language knows
where rust ends
salmon, pink begin

I tell you
landscape is truer than you
less curt
and more careless

        space

        and so who
        was the city's mother? did it
        have one? or who
        taught the city
        to cleanse itself so well?
        red buses are licked
        clean as a whistle
        by starving commuters
        tube trains smarter than hoovers
        gulp up dollops of junk — whoosh
        now you see them — whoosh
        now you don't
        and autumn streets
        which should be flossy with joy
        have their deep soft toffee drifts
        eaten by yellow machines

        no-one will let me
        come to them
        along steps a nimble neat man
        very gently he tells me
        my open door is obscene

        no
        the city has only a father
        with a gold moustache and a chain

and a stop-
watch for a heart
he made this city, he planned it
his logic laid out squares
as cold as himself
those cocksure terrible towers
those tidy ticketed lusts
he patented them, he made public
his architecture of ice

the moon has been exiled
along with daughters and plants
the moon rocks by in a merry blue flood
the moon throws silver all over me
she says beware

beware of hunger, caresses
beware the time of bleeding
the shapes of bellies, of breasts

beware unruliness

Eve, etcetera

eve, etcetera
filthy whores the lot of them

generations later
there is so much dirt
I must dispose of: my
sick unsteady heart
screeching in the night
my grabbing mouth, desire
that won't let go, needs
deep as a pit, and darker
anger breaking like a red rash
over and over again

I screen myself
under the white dress of a communicant
I seal my lips with safety pins
now I am ready
never to write a love poem

I have been wanting to mourn

I have been wanting
to mourn for a long time
to mourn for a past time
the bells of the ambulance this morning
beat at my head like angry fists
beat up my heart if I let them

in the French village of my childhood
each death, a steeple
rocked with our grief
so we assembled, we knew
who was meant, the bells told us
a clang for each year of the life
the black copes of the priests
blotted our bright tears
we sang rejoicing, God
had eaten another of us
we were still
his obedient children

years later in England
relatives began being
ticked off at Golders Green crematorium
meat out of the fridge
and into the fire
we prayed, our lips
stiff as the corpse
we were too young to see

and there have been friends
three of them
dead by suicide
I have hung their carcases in my throat

I want a funeral first
where I can mourn
mothering, and mourn
me, losing and lost, I
wanting her cradle
fat gobbler of gaps
and of anger, my consolation
the grave shovelled into my mouth

I have found women
to witness my loss
of blood of mother of childhood
called puberty (that is all
the word should be larger than that)
I call myself woman, I try to
it means accepting such pain:
no-one can ever love me
like that
nevermore
oh no never again

PAT VAN TWEST

'if you have the courage to speak out what you are you will find you are not alone" / inspires me still / my eldest son took the photo to celebrate my recent fortieth birthday / there have been many exciting beginnings and / i foresee more . . .

when you accuse me of not being
like a woman
i wonder what like is
& how one becomes it.

i think woman is what
women are
& as i am one
so must that be included
in what woman is

So, therefore, i am like.

poem to my son

are you weary of the whining edge of wind
that signifies I am the mother
who thrust you forth?
it is an interminable truth from which there is no escaping
like your face
I understand your screwballed nose, tongue-poked insult
what a business, coming to terms with it all
from what god-blasted cloud did you fall?
but if we are talking of perplexity
I can match yours with the skill of a trained saleslady matching wool
I have nestled the caress of the thought of you
into the hollowness of my hand
holding the ten-years-old of you
I am a stranger still to my mothercraft
and
I do not know you at all.

   that summer
we shall say
do you remember that summer . . .
when we reached my first festival in the end
after running out of petrol & siphoning some off in a village
with the impossible name of Clutton
and you took cocoa in your ridiculous hat
and smiled your smile of complicity
being the born bitch that you are
whilst the wife of the man who was siphoning
entertained us with her special ignorance
and you said afterwards
wasnt she a gas
whilst i could only think of her dreary life
not wanting to believe she was really happy
like you said . . .
and my first festival received me with its open arms
swallowing my voracious virginity in one gulp
and you smiled, hoping i'd run into a naked hells angel
in the region of the macrobiotic tent . . .

you sat decorated by suave sophistication
and i learnt that you'd never be a dab with a billy-can

I'm made for the best hotels i think you said
i threw another image of you away
& trod it underfoot all the way to the plastic pyramid
a few nudes and a fuck later i returned to your aura
of respectable foyers and posh previews
and we left behind my first festival. I hadn't done one freaky thing
except perhaps arrive there with you
and that summer, we shall say
when we wore our mauve gay liberation badges everywhere
though we were not yet gay
when you taught me about messages on the juke-box
and we conversed in numbers
A7 i said love love me do
F4 you answered It dont come easy
and that summer when we first treated seriously the idea of living with
                                          another woman
and you made schemes to get rich quick
and i left it all to you because i made a point of not understanding money
in order to keep up the right anarchist image . . .
that summer when we stopped shooting off our mouths about important
                                      things'
and found that life was, after all, happening nowhere else
but where we were . . .
that summer
do you
remember . . .
?

Will I Wither?

What inner eye turns blind
in a woman. Forced to askance
so its function
fails lest the test of its scrutiny
screams : not me not me!
We all have seen them. Why
do we think we shall not be one?
Do we think they were never young
born with their wrinkles?

No consolation I
have always preferred
the shrivelled skin of old apples
their resistance lower
maybe they are thankful
for the devouring bite that promises an end
to it all. No juice but a tired flesh.
The touch of my mother's cheek never fails to move me.

We are the dumb waiters
never daring to answer fate back
for its cruelty. Old age is laughable
there is no escaping it.
We act as if it only happens to others
& as for women — even Nature laughs
up her sleeve at her ultimate
unfairness; taking away the fecund
that all our lives kept us inferior.

Nin-hur-sa-ga, Sister Silbury.

for us
the obstetricians
she moves not
gives up secrets
only to the initiated
skulduggery nor
higher authority
cannot replace
our midwifery
a transverse caesarean section
reveals no embryo
full term she causes conception
this birth we are witnessing
requires but
patience the skill

over the brow of an eastward hill
this still

placid belly

suddenly
i am delivered a brain child
doubtless
i am destined
to complete this minutes madness

the journey is quieter now
the way to go is known
if enough of you came it could be comforting
if enough of us went we would be sanity.

PAULA JENNINGS

*Born into patriarchy 1950. Reborn into feminism 1971. Being born ever since.
I think poems are like dreams and are the nearest thing we've got to a woman's
way of expressing through writing. They're like a crystal-clear jumble of feelings
and pictures and contradictions. They say in a few words what male, straight-line
thinking would take pages to say and still get wrong. I write poems because it
gives me a sort of controlled-hysterical feeling that I like. I don't write specific-
ally to communicate but they tend to be easy to understand and make women
laugh. That's nice.*

The Perfumed Garden
or
A Lesbian Ghetto Isn't Good Enough

Rest.
See, the marigold cups her honey arms
about her still centre.
The tree, huge and certain, shrugs the wind;
bean blossom bursts her scarlet into pods for you.

Rest.
See, the lupin pepper-scents the garden,
her green hands wide open.

Lavender aims her sprigs brave at the sun;
passionflowers cartwheel under the glass for you.

Rest?
How can I rest with this patriarchal rose bush
up my arse?

⏣ You rush in with a face like spring
      and firmly press your heart into my hand.

            "No, really, it's so very big and new
            and red and throbbing
            and my hand doesn't look quite comfortable.
            Besides, it burns."

         "Oh, but it suits you,
          honestly, it looks good
          and you'll soon get used to the warmth."

            "Well, perhaps some other time . . ."

         "At least give it a·try,
          take a risk for once."

            "Perhaps I am being a bit silly . . .
            Actually it feels more comfortable now
            and the warmth *is* rather nice . . .
            Hey, what are you doing?"

         "Well, there's this friend, see,
          she definitely likes hearts —
          I'll bring it back" . . . . . .

            ⏣ Leadenflower moon spitting silver.
                 So many tides dragging thick blood undertow,
                 womb blood, warm blood,
                 moving to a spring tide.

Lesbian

Your petals open wet
to cradle my fingers
and I think tomorrow
I will scrawl
in red paint
on the town hall
that behind the word lesbian
stinking in men's mouths,
rhyming with perversion and revulsion,
was always this word
with a soft 'l' like in laughter and lilac
and an 's' that tenderness dissolves into
as your petals open wet
to cradle my fingers.

Dressed to Kill

Yes, I realise my baggy dungarees
just make the shape of my bum
more mysterious
and my wellies might hold a certain allure
for rubber fetishists
and my hair (unbrushed for a week)
looks untamed
and my fat jumper simply emphasizes
my essential femininity

but

if you don't take your slimey masculine eyes
off me
I will whip out the collapsible submachine gun
I always carry in my sexy old haversack
and blast you off the face of the earth.

Just thought I'd mention it.

PAULINE LONG

At dawn on the summer solstice in 1978 I watched the sun break through at the stone circle at Arbor Low, Derbyshire. There was an exaltation of skylarks, rising vertically, motivated by the sound they make. I feel myself in the women's movement with the sounds I make, and hope some of them are heard and find echoes in women's beings. I believe our sisterhood is whole and indivisible, each of us perhaps making different noises, but the aim is that we should all make our own noise. Blessed be.

If women could speak, what language would they use? Part II

If you go walking in a wood in winter,
And speak to the stones, half buried in the snow
Watch twirling leaves and dry sticks floating
Tread into muddy bracken, see still branches,
Thin skeletons of bodies yet to flourish,

If you go walking in a winter forest
Hear me, sisters, hear me speak again

If you go walking in your silence
Stretching your skin to the cold air
Stomaching your silence, your acquiescence, your solicitude,

Bearing your guilt, the guilt of too little patience,
Your guilt of the wish to speak,
Of the wish for a tear of loving,
A tear of communion you know can never happen

If you go walking, sister, in a wood in winter
Stumbling into mud, knee-high,
Vision a bird scuttling, then flying,
Winging on to a low horizon;

As I shall speak, my words are meant for you.
For you sister, weeping in the long grass,
For you sister, lying on a hard bed
For you, sister, whispering, hoping, playing, praying,
Whimpering, imploring, shrilly crying
Burning with a hard guilt,
Silent and screaming out your silence.

Who are you, dear sister, image,
Dressed and undressed, to play, to pay, to be made nothing of,
To be made into nothing, to become no-one
To keep silence?

Find a half-buried stone and rest there;
Stand in the stone's huge shadow and rest there;
Hide in the stone's curved form and rest there;
Hear the stones speak for me and rest there.

I was everything who went down into nothing,
They wrenched my earth and my moon, drowned me into nothing,
To be forgotten, to be annihilated from time,
To be no-one, nowhere, no person
No voice.

I do not exist.

Except in the hard pain in your body,
The clench at the heart,
Head throbbing, high pitch of tears,
The bruise, the cut, the stumble, the bowed head,
The silence.

              * *   * *   * *

Who are those women, standing there and laughing,
Those women standing there, dancing,
Those women, singing, talking, speaking, shouting,

Speaking in some language that some understand
Speaking with eyes and tongue and head and body
Speaking.

Who are those women, speaking out, in some language
Singing with music of flute and strings,
Walking in spirals through the stone circles,
Shouting, in my mazes?

Shall the moon see, shall the moon rise
The serpents move in unison, the snails in circle,
The goats sing
Again?

Shall the stones whistle, bound in harmony,
To be heard, to be contemplated, to be reciprocated.

Shall the slit throat be healed,
To let sound through
And the breath come noisily?

    Women, defend me.
I am the dark river bearing your flowers.
Defend me

I am the night where the dead live,
The luminous heart of the dark
Where glistens a whirl of day,
Defend me.

Your voice is my white seed of creation,
That I dropped into the garden,

Your voice is the cauldron
That brews knowledge

Your voice is the satisfied sigh of a contented child;
The volcano of ecstasy;

Your voice that speaks in language
(That more understand)
Defends me.

Brings me up through the thick earth to smile on my daughters.
Who are me.

Blessed Be.

SALLY BERRY

Born and lived the first 25 years in Oklahoma, USA. Then travelled and worked in the Philippines, Germany and England. Have been living in London for the past 7 years and working as a psychotherapist.

I have been writing for as long as I can remember but it took the support, encouragement and understanding I found in my women writers' group to enable me to share my writing.

I scream
    You read your book
I scream again
    You turn the page

I am dying
    You are reading
I want more than this
    You turn the page

It was more
More than
Blows
Screams
Anger
Hatred
Jealousy

I saw
And
Can not forget

I saw the look
Upon a face
That wanted
To smash Me
Out of being

I saw
And
Can not forget

Perhaps
I should understand
It was not to me
The anger
Was really directed

And yet
the bruises are
on my arms

I have pretended
Lack of knowledge
Even sealed
My eyes shut
To keep the Knowing Out

I have shouted
I have wept
All to keep sound
Filling the air
To push back
The silence that
The knowing is

By a thread
I'm held
I thought to follow
the thread
Unravel the knots
that are my life
I carefully traced
And suddenly saw
By a thread
I'm held
And I choose
You as scissors

I am sitting in a room
It is a narrow room
Suddenly I realize
The walls are moving towards each other
Now I can only get through
by moving sideways
One wall is pressing my back
the other my stomach
there is just enough space
for me to reach the door
I move through an ever narrowing space
toward a door I know not where it leads
[Is this a dream?]

⧖ The time seems long
Since I left that other world
Where you are now

In my mind I move
Through that world
Seeking you in thought

There is so much
I want to say
But am afraid of not knowing the language

It has taken this journey
Back to my beginning
To unravel so many knots

I have learned
That I do love you
But what I have sought you can not give

What must be done I am unsure
But that I must find it
I know

Loving can warm me
But it can not stop
The cold pain

The pain I must
Face and name
But it can begin

⧖ I knew the quicksand was there
You were walking ahead
I said
'Be careful'
You said: 'Leave me alone
You always interfere'
I said again
A warning 'Take Care'
You said 'Don't bother me
Leave me alone, alone'
Then you stepped into
The quicksand
And I left you alone

SHEILA ROWBOTHAM

*I was born in 1943 in Leeds & educated at a Methodist school near Filey,
Yorkshire and St. Hilda's College Oxford 1961-1964. I worked in technical
colleges, further education and schools. I now teach for the Workers'
Educational Association. I am a socialist involved in the women's movement
since it began in Britain. I live with a group of friends in Hackney, London and
I have a son who will be 2 in March 1979.* I have written, Women, Resistance
and Revolution *(Penguin)*, Woman's Consciousness, Man's World *(Penguin)*,
Hidden from History *(Pluto)*, A New World for Women, Stella Brown Socialist
Feminist *(Pluto), with Jeff Weeks* Socialism and the New Life *(Pluto), with Jean
McCrindle edited* Dutiful Daughters *(Penguin). I have contributed poetry to*
Cutlasses and Earrings.

253 Bus — Hackney to Whitechapel

The old women on the bus,
fat with poverty and processing
have a kind of shiny pallor
and mistrust,
swollen ankles,
no shapedness,
bunched veins bulging
on marked flesh.

Socks over stockings,
their legs are straddled on the sideways seat
apart.
Their thighs thrust through suspenders,
bellies sagging,
clutching baskets at their breasts.

What do they remember?

The role of Women in the Revolution defined by some Socialist men (1968)

Let us put pin-ups in the Black Dwarf
Let us wank into Revolution

Let us find girls to make the tea
Let us explain to them
The nature and limits of emancipation

Let us stick cunts
On our projecting egos
Calling this comradeship
And the end of exploitation

Let us decorate our killing
By screwing all the women

Let us have pretty girls on the platform
Of our revolution

Let us play with the mangled bodies
Of the women of Vietnam

Let us marry young wives
In order to sell our line

And leave her rotting corpse
To float forgotten
Down the river
Of OUR revolution

My Friend

My friend
cooks sweet
apples
far into
the night.

A gift
of gentleness
through time,
country kitchens
in the sun
perfume
the dark
still.

Their fragrance
lingers
until
light.

The sad tale of nobody me

who told me to paddle my own canoe
into the sewer
of once begun
who told me too many cocks collide
into the pantry
and make some jam
who told me the gift horse
spits in your face
who told me his cock
chops into my head
in for a sheep and in for a lamb
grab the penny and grab the pound
make a ring and all go round

nobody's world is falling down
and nobody told
so nobody knew
while nobody paddled her own canoe.

SHEILA SHULMAN

Born in 1936, grew up in Brooklyn. My family were East European Jewish immigrants who struggled to stay alive. I have inherited most of their fears and some of their determination. I came to feminism late and reluctantly, having been sucker enough to think that humanism and left politics did include me. I unlearned a lot (the hard way), learned a lot, eventually (also the hard way). I'm still doing both. I could not have written anything had I not been for five years part of a women's writers' group who encouraged, prodded, warmed me into beginning to find my own voice(s). I'm a lesbian, a feminist, and by conviction and economic necessity, a printer. I live in England because I became all of those here.

Pome for Jackie

You would understand about Brooklyn
and my grandmother's house,
the hour or two of peace
on Friday before
the Queen turned away in disgust
at my uncles, their pinochle and cigars.

My grandmother and I sometimes
were quiet in the afternoon

as she baked the Sabbath bread
or sniffled tearfully
onto her ironing
over the soap-operas in Yiddish
that lamented how the "Golden Land"
wasn't, after all.

Piles of bedclothes
aired in the open windows,
all the rooms steamed
with the good smells of food
that was, I guess,
her only way of loving.

I hung around the kitchen
trying to get her to tell me stories
of before she came to America,
amazed at her hands, suddenly delicate,
plaiting the ropes of dough for the bread.

We both know the sadness
of how it wasn't quite like that,
wasn't quite that simple,
or even if it was,
what was wrong with it all, anyway:
mothers and daughters blind to each other,
stunned   like oxen by their uncleanness.

We know the peculiar pain
of being an exile,
even from the diaspora,
with really no place to go.
Our memories are very long;
sometimes I think I inherited
generations of memories of memories
before anyone told me anything.

It's always been the music's held me
when all the rest was bankrupt and betrayed.
I love the wild, the aching gaiety,
forced like a spring from rock,
and sure, it's sad music, mostly,
but I'm grateful for tears
that pelt down like summer rain,
and so might they have been,
those old people I always imagine

dancing at weddings
in a strange country, choked
on the bitterness of exile and poverty.

Our exile's different,
we're not starving,
but see, here we are
coming home at last
to our own bodies,
paring away slowly, in pain,
all the selves we aren't,
finding, in pain, and some joy,
all the selves we are,
meeting at last as women, simply.

We've lost nothing,
and how would I have found you,
my sister,
if we had not, each of us,
turned our backs
on all that seemed safe, said,
I have no name, no place, no past,
I will begin again.

When I say (meaning you) "my sister",
some childhood loneliness is healed.
And when we meet now, too seldom,
for me it's coming home,
not to the one we remember
(though that one's there as well)
but to the one we're building now,
made up of many lives, many places,
and all
the holy sparks of love and life
that sometimes light our way.

⬙ now, as I begin to age
now, as I learn to be alone
now my body begins to be alive

there is no way
to make up for lost time
I cannot bear to lose any more

I feel the life in my veins
and my empty hands
and my urgency

I have fought hard
I have been healed
(but not quite)

so my lovers will be women
for whom loving women
is already a clear and
bedrock passion

women to whom
I am simply another woman
like themselves

not a symbol
of a breakthrough
or breakout
or crossing a line

not an experience
on the basis of which
they will make a decision
about their sexuality
or politics
or both

not an experiment
in expanded consciousness
or comparative eroticism

simply another woman
lover   sister   friend

✠   for years I slept in the same room
as my mother   every morning
I saw her wake up   lie silently awhile
struggle stiffly out of bed   struggle
to get her girdle on   saw the fat
on her waist   her ass   her thighs
squeezed mercilessly
saw her pull on her dress   groan
as she bent to put on her shoes
grimace into a mirror   pluck
a few hairs from her chin   (I
do that now)   put on
her makeup   her scarf   her hat   her coat
drink coffee standing   leave for work

the same gestures   every day for years
only stiffening
she was in pain   I found her graceless

I hated it when she called me
to the bathroom   to speak to me
while she was in the shower
her body repelled me
her broad freckled back
looked beaten
her scarred belly sagged
(I'd been a caesarian   and she often said
I wasn't worth the trouble)
she was flabby and worn

the flat was small
we watched television a lot
she talked   I had nothing to say
as she said   you could have cut the air with a knife

every night   I lay in bed   imagining
vividly   in intricate detail
all the ways I could kill her
or myself   anything that would stop that sound
as she   snored her exhaustion out

some nights   she didn't fall asleep
she spoke the perpetual litany of her aborted life
our uneasy bodies   found what comfort they could
I covered my head with the pillow   she repeated
that I was   an ungrateful bitch

216

that I had no heart   that although
I read so many books
I didn't know my ass from my elbow
that I was killing her   while
she was killing herself for me
that my only friend   was
taking advantage of me   was using me
for some unknown purpose of her own
and anyway I couldn't trust a friend

then she begged me   to confide in her

she wanted a normal daughter   married
with kids   a house   a good life
she got me   she tried   I tried
neither of us had a chance

My body's long memory still makes trouble

I do not dance   I do not know
what it feels like   from inside   to dance
I stand   I look   my body
does not move   more than is necessary
I am heavy   my flesh is dead weight
but I ache   I ache

for two or three years   once
I stole all of my mother's coins   daily
I bought Italian sandwiches
made of half a loaf of bread   and
bags of broken slabs of chocolate
ate it all   my
later behaviour is not so different
I sweat with shame

I am afraid to touch anyone
I am gross   they will shudder
I am clumsy   I will hurt
I cannot bear to touch myself
no one touches me

I see myself all the time
flabby legs   bulging gut
thick waist   I try to
turn my eyes away   but
even the young trees   hurt them

I am saturated with novels   with
poetry   with half the literature
of the known world   and probably
all of its advertising   all of which
tells me   I can only exist   as
a caricature   a reject   a minor character
and as I am a woman
it's even worse than that

"You're so fat who'd wanna rape you?"

HARD WORDS or, Why Lesbians Have to be Philosophers

I

queer   bent   deviant   sick
perverted   abnormal   unnatural

I keep telling myself   that these words
which I have difficulty typing   because
I have not yet completely unlearned
that they describe me   have the power they do
only in relation to a cluster of
assumptions theories hypotheses and illuminations
collectively regarded by the whole human community
as   the real world   or   the natural order
otherwise known as   the straight and narrow

I have had to become more independent
and differ on this point
from the whole human community
(an awkward position but you do understand)

now I no longer know what the natural order is
or even if there is one   but if there is
it does/will have to include me
even if I have to create it

II

those words up there are   as it were
an ontological charge   brought by the world
in the persons of various mediators   who
could be anybody   philosophers   priests   scientists
teachers   doctors   your mother   or your friend
and ultimately   of course   yourself

a charge of which you are invariably
guilty until proven innocent   (that depends
on whether you co-operate)
the penalty is excommunication   and it can be
retroactive

III

queer   bent   deviant   sick
perverted   abnormal   unnatural

the women I know   who live with men
(whether there's one around or not is not germane)
do not (they say)   feel that way   about us
who live with women
(I do not know what they say to their men
or to each other   or think to themselves)

nevertheless   they are uneasy
nevertheless   they keep their men in tow
nevertheless   they choke on "lesbian"
(bisexual is a much more palatable word)

yet they are very curious
as if about an alien life form
ripples of confused erotic energy
dance at us   across the line
that they/we have drawn

they know we are safe   that
we will not make trouble because
we are   of course
sensitive to their needs   (good friends we are)
which are not for us   not that way

their needs are for men and children and houses
for being part of what they think has always been
the natural order   world without end

each of them however fights to keep
a little patch clear   (that's where we come in)
for their wildness to grow in   safely
they want   fully covered risks
a contradiction in terms   if ever I heard one

they have never discovered
that insurance is a racket

IV

they are all good liberals
and there is so much *real* suffering
we are neither (literally) starving   nor
(literally) dying   except for some of us
but they are only suicides   nor (yet)
political prisoners   nor (physically) tortured

we are (as far as they know)   middle-class
well-educated   decently housed and fed   and
not visibly oppressed   (not   say   like blacks)
moreover we live in a morally permissive society
in which no one much cares
who goes to bed with whom   or why
so what is all the fuss about

they are good liberals
their hearts are in the right place
their minds are open
they would even consider . . .   well . . .   perhaps . . .
how admirable   how easy

they cannot be expected to understand
much less to share
the urgencies of women who   because
they have forfeited even the slave-quarters
forfeited even their tenuous right to exist
as an unfortunate biological necessity
consequently do not exist at all

or   since we do go on being around
exist only as a grotesque anomaly   a sterile affront
to a harmonious natural world
quite possibly   a danger   and   almost certainly
a threat to their precarious equilibrium

how can they share our urgencies when
sharing them would mean recognizing that
the only difference   between us and them
is that   in return for certain services
their men grant them a dubious protection
and throw them a metaphysical bone
which allows them to think   that they too
are part of the world

V

now we know more about where we stand
and why that line is there
why I am a lot more anxious than they are
about the nature of things
the relation of the human to the natural   and
what transformations of   the real world   are possible

either the world is going to move over
and make plenty of room for me
or it's going to choke on me   but
it's not going to spit me out

they say to me   on behalf of the world
but there is plenty of room
their generosity is presumptuous

no one speaks to me on behalf of the world
I am the world   as they are
indigenous wildlife   see   like trees
and dolphins   and children
as innocent   as natural   and perhaps
though I'm sure they can hardly stomach the thought
more human   because   necessarily
more conscious
think about that for awhile

STEF PIXNER

Born London 1945. lives with friends in Hackney, London. works as a poly-
technic lecturer. has been writing poetry since age eleven. has written songs for
women's movement events, and contributed fiction, reviews, and drawings to
Spare Rib. joined a women writers' group in 1977. we gave each other the
confidence to publish a book of our own poems: "Licking the Bed Clean".

high heeled sneakers

i dreamed Simone de Beauvoir and i
were climbing a mountain eating crepes
and wearing espadrilles. she carried
her alarm clock on her head
whereas i pulled behind me three train
carriages full of the things i thought
i might need for the journey.
we talked pleasantly of this and that. i
was trying to impress her with how
interesting i was coming from the post
war generation from a communist family
and being a woman but i had to stop
every now and again to change my

espadrilles for ballet shoes or army boots
or pick my nose or adjust a comma
on my hat or look at the view
or a word in the dictionary so that
she got to the top of the mountain before
me despite her years and
ate more crepes in the meanwhile
sitting on her alarm clock and waiting
for me and my train. when i got
there at last she said there are some
questions i've been meaning
to ask a woman of your
gencration and so she began asking me
questions and i changed from my
army boots to a pair of high heeled
sneakers and back to espadrilles and then
back into ballet shoes. i've been meaning
to write you a long letter i said but just
then we saw a horde of mountain bears make
off with the luggage i'd so carefully
chosen and she still had a few books
to eat that morning so we exchanged
espadrilles and chinese postcards and
waved our red handkerchiefs
just as the lights went up.

the pain that i find in dust and disorder

the pain that i find
in dust and disorder
she carries on her back
like bread.

i asked for a ladder
for a gilded stagecoach
i asked for the moon

i found old tins in the cupboard
old tins, old dust
and her soft, soft skin.

fox colours of rust and brown
a nest of yellowed papers
and a bed full of books.

she gave me bunches
of words on a keyring
and question marks
to open locked doors.

the pain that i find
in dust and disorder
she carries on her back
like bread.

THAT WORLD THROUGH THE WINDOW IS A BAREFACED LIE

that world
through the window
is a barefaced lie.

there is ink on the yellow fields
and the moon
has been glued to the night
like an egg in a scrapbook.

bitter the battering moth
and the grasses that wind
shaken wave.

bitter the bird that flies
in ever smaller circles
as the poisoned world contracts.

there is a cold wind
inside me
and a bird
flies like a black rag
over the fields
behind my eyes.

the weeds the witch and the roses

tonight
i shouted at you
i shouted at your back

you said nothing
i was behind you
behind you on the same bed

outside snow was falling

january.

twentyone years ago
we hid in the weeds
        under the witch
        among the roses

schoolgirls in blue and grey
there was you and me
the weeds the witch and the roses

the ghost
in our impossible machine
tracked us
twentyone winters,
the machine we invented
to fool the others

our secrets bound us
now they're out.

STEPHANIE MARKMAN

born in 1952. living in edinburgh. first story: 'janetta the puppet who came to life' 1961 (now lost). currently writing a 140-verse poem, 'the rime of the ancient feminist', halfway through and still limping on. heavily into rhyming.

 and
mother why did you tell me
tell me
tell me why did you lie
mother why did you teach me
teach me
to watch through a veil of fears
and where is the garden mother
i can't see the garden any more
i can feel the grass
oh i can feel the grass
but i can't see the air
no i can't see the air
i can't see the
oh i can't see no i can't
not through this veil of —

oh and why
do you mystify me so mother
twist me and bereave me

and drag me dancing up this
garden path of yours
i'd like my own garden path mother
when can i be old enough
bold enough
told enough
to lead myself up
up my
very own garden

and long time ago now mother
you were my garden
i watched with you your sky
we saw
eye to eye
and do you blame me
blame me
if i've trampled in my panic
all your nicely tended ways
is it my fault
my fault mother
that your grass has turned to straw

and yes i remember
that a rose by any other
mother
and yes you told me
that the grass is always
greener
and is it my fault
my fault
that i've pushed beyond your railings
do you blame me
blame me mother
if a weed is just a flower
growing in the wrong garden

and if only
i could walk
through this veil of fears
if my eyes weren't
cataracts
from your unshed tears
then i would in my gratitude
cry

that perhaps you didn't lie
mother
just wanted to see your vision
in my eyes
no lies mother
just bad dreams.

just a minute
a minute a minute
I'm talking I'm
talking I'm talking
I'm talking

father
of all the minutes
wasted
it is these I mourn
all these small dead selves
hulking, skulking
at the foot of your patriarchal table

even my mother
would have me eat
but not you
no not you
no
the woman giveth
and the man
taketh
taketh
taketh away

and you come at me
like death
who denies
who can't let be

you come at me
full of your father's death
full of your own death
full of my dying

you come at me
like death
that final paterfamilias

and it's too late
too late
for asking permission
too many minutes are lost
it's too late
too late
to wait for your blessing

in silence
I leave the table.

odd
is what you said
it's very odd

it was too

odd to be there
you with your eyes
half closed
in surprised sensuality
your face hovering
a little above mine

and who'd have thought it
who'd have thought it
who'd seen us so carefully friends
I'd have thought it
yes I'd have thought it
but I'd never
no never
have said

but odd
you said
as I smiled
as you smiled
with relief

odd.

THALIA DOUKAS

I cannot escape, I observe the world through a feminist lens: I wear feminist glasses. What I read, what I see in art or life, the way I evaluate my actions or state — refer back to feminist considerations. Tensions and conflicts are feminist: where does this put women? what does it say about women? are women "reduced" or "enlarged" in this connection or context?

I write because I seem to be compelled to remark, sift, pin certain things down, get past what I ought to think or feel and confront what I believe must be true especially about myself, people close to me, particular experiences I've had. Since what I write works best in brief, succinct words, it's most easily described as poetry — although I am not so much trying to create literature; I am trying to speak.

Rowing practice

I row for you,
though the dinghy
goes in circles,
stuck to the center
of a flat lake
fringed with pointed
evergreens in a
deep shadow ring

'round the reflected
moon and assembled
milky clouds. You
are shadows on a
distant shore, patient but
keen to see when, or if,
I'll row a straight course.
You'd wait forever
it appears, standing
always, never
speaking:

it fills me with tears, not
to see you come close
or hear a chorus
of cheers.

Falling on nails

Is it
falling on nails?
Do you go
pulling it from you
like so many nails,
nettles, bloodied feathers?
Do you become like some
demented bird, pulling
feathers from your breast,
if you let it come too close?
Does it beckon you forward
while holding you back
'til your head rolls
to corners from which
it's not easily retrieved?
Do you recall
the other day, when sails filled
the river and hedges were green
domes, not palace garden mazes,
and clocks wore hands and faces?

Does time melt
out of shape?

Is it
while scratching some initials
into a painted sill, with a
quill pen from a stray
feather, that Escape
becomes Resolving to Go?
Does your mouth smile
and do you shiver,
making a lopsided
way to the
exit?

Fighting a notion

Fighting a notion to yield,
an urge to be taken or towed
on water skis by a mythical
sea beast in tropical sun
and bracing salt breeze,
to music. (It's no destiny,
it simply hits like fate.)
Resisting calmly,
until a winding down,
like the slowing of a wristwatch.

("It's feeding
on itself; it's
fighting back,"
a voice from
nowhere
advises.)

No trusting or taking-up
this yearning to be borne —
helpless, spaniel-like,
open-mouthed, —
away.

I will
roll the wise fist.
Retreat. Refrain from following.
Unlock the armour.
Step in its cool shell.

It's a knocking down,
over and out, a roll-
ing flat, wafer thin;
like fossils in stone:

going back to
being complete
alone.

Blood order

To see real blood, men travel
men travel miles
to the city,
jungle or
desert, hazarding
boredom and disease.
For blood's sake,
they endure tight
uniforms, all in
patriotic colours:
blood is different,
for women.
In teaspoon or
cupfuls, it measures
the love-making and
child-making;
all women are members
of the order of
blood which
sometimes
unpredictably
alters their lives,
marks their time.
To join the blood order,
men require cunning,
take risks on sports
grounds, simulate it
for entertainment,
devise methods in rural
settings for killing
rabbits, foxes, bears.
To be close to fresh
red-flowing blood is
costly, cooperative
effort, when men rob a
bank, hi-jack an air-
plane, harpoon a whale.
It can be exotic,
seeping in tropical
corners in shadows,
or across latin borders,
or aboard ships at sea.

But, bleeding is solitary
and domesticated, for
women. Their
blood rites are
enacted at
home, discreetly,
often on white,
pale pink or
baby blue
tiles.

Table talk

My dear,
at his table
we did not speak.
We ducked.
We ducked as
soup tins and
cereal boxes,
pots, pans, army shoe-
shine kits, coins, the
entire meal, the house-
hold effects, briefcase,
black Royal typewriter,
file cabinets, bills,
bicycles, the car,
lawn mower, weedkiller,
turntable, slide pro-
jector, movie machines,
airplanes, battleships,
the G. I. Bill, her
best shoes,
chocolate boxes,
baseball bats,
back brace,
bridge,
the moustache of
Groucho Marx, all
c a t a p u l t e d
past, skimming the stuff
on our backs, making our
hair fly in many
directions.

I tell you,
even now, when
I see a fork
or a folded napkin,
the palms of my hands
go damp-ice cold.

SIX

One

My chest opens
little swiss doors.

The cuckoo rolls
out on wheel-feet
and sings, full
enough to pop.

Full enough so
my heart might
stop,
I warble as
the clock strikes,
and keen observers
note angular
bulbs,
housed inside my
blouse.

Two

Inside my chest
I rise like dough,
I expand, I swell,
I stock a fullness
hard to suppress or
evade or hide:
I unlock
my larder
and the loaf
sleeps
inside,
rising.

(The cuckoo
has its nest
on the top.)

Three

I am so full I
am a dozen eggs
cracking open,
releasing
a dozen sparrows
with wings alight,
all taking flight,
beating the air,
a dozen pounding
bird hearts,
awful, suspended
in white flames,
scattering
ash,
consumed.

Four

I am a drab grey bird
trapped in a kitchen,
trying to alight
on red hot rings
of
an
electric
range.

Five

I am scattered.
I am scattered
ash.
I am dust.
I am so full,
I am a fine dust
and ashes,
spilling like surf
from every window
in this house,
in-
sisting.

Six

I am an
egg inside
an egg
inside an
egg inside
an egg
inside an
egg inside
an egg
inside an
egg inside
an egg
inside an
egg inside
an egg
inside an
egg inside
an egg.

VALERIE SINASON

*Born in 1946 my teens were in the early 60's on a London council estate where wo
woman was either pure and sedentary (stilettoes were not good running shoes),
fast (cheap and guilty) and my mode of being was seen as "tomboy". Several
poems here reflect that experience. Since being involved with feminism and
poetry publishing (Gallery magazine) I have taken delight in the growing accept-
ance of different kinds of creative expression and ways of living. The poem here
that matters most to me is about my two grandmothers and the writing resolved
a lot of confused feelings.*

Passing the Test

There were six of them coming
and the big one had an airgun
pointed at me
and the zips on their jackets
were trapping the light.

Yvonne said "Run!"
and I ran fastest,
over snake traps and stag beetles,
over the farmer's land,
his dogs barking like gunshot.

And then up my tree,
heart loud as bird cry
hair catching in the bark.

But the big one called
"You're gonna get done"
and he started to climb.

And the second one,
the one with brylcreem matting his hair,
unzipped his trousers.
"Got something to show you"
he called.

So I climbed higher and higher
the sky spinning like a top
and I was so high up
and crowned with leaves
and they looked so small
so very small

I just laughed

And my laughter plaited
with sunlight and leaf
and their stones missed me
and their pellets went past me

And the big one jumped down
his hand torn by branches,
his flick-knife,
a flashing arc against the sun,
blunting,
stuck in the bark.

And I just sat
the sun skipping round my head
all green and golden
until the glitter left their zips
until they went away
their shoulders shrivelled as dead leaves.

Until Yvonne returned with Ed
who said I could join his gang
even though I was only a girl

And I climbed down the tree
like a queen descending velvet stairs
and decided to ask for an air pistol for Christmas.

There was once a woman . . .

It is time for the touching of foreheads
the farewell of mindprints.
She is passing through her third skin
so clear and fragile now.

through her glass breasts
the cracked blood turns to leave her
the heartbeat drums in on itself

she is passing through the Road of Changing Faces
in search of Signs.

A woman in Spanish dress
lies on a stretcher in a sunny garden
she waves a white handkerchief three times.

Her black mantilla
is the smoke
above the stake
at the centre of the world.

Was that it? Was it then?
With bonfires of women
lighting the way
down the Road of the Burning Years.

She takes a wisp of smoke to herself.
Between her legs the gas-ovens roar.
It was not the sign she wanted.

She is passing back, further back,
the great golden warrior women
slice off a breast for the curve of the giant bow.
In the round pool
their muscles quiver and tense.

Was that it? Was it then?
She trembles at their approach
weak as the boychild left on the mountains.

She reaches for two torn breasts,
in her hands they change colour and size.
She does not know the true sign.
She is journeying through the ventre of the nipple

Eve, she calls, Mary, she calls, Athena, she calls.

She is burning on the cross
on the centrefold of the sky
her breasts as pink as a sacrificial pig.

Isis! she calls. Kali! she calls. Shiva! she calls.

The smoke weaves her a black nun's habit,
the smoke weaves her a black negligee
her child burns a black hole in her womb
her eyelashes are black, her lips flame red.

There was once a woman, she screams, a woman . . .
She is passing through her third skin.

Dressed to be killed
(an angry response to the high court judge who acquitted a man of
rape saying the woman was "dressed to kill")

This is for all of us sisters,
in boots, sandals, stockings, tights,
bras, braless, concealed, revealed,

Because, Your Honour,
we are always dressed to be killed.

Even the Nun in the funny posters
with her black tights exposed.
All open to hate messages from a phallic pen.

"Whore", he yelled,
"Witch-bitch", he bawled,
that man leering outside the pub.
And I wonder what red-hot womb curse
I can stir for him.

May nipples stick in his throat
and shut his loveless mouth.
May giant pincered vaginas
loom behind him and corner him
in a dark alleyway,
May every night shadow
be a womb out to drown him.

But,
because my monsters were taught to weep,
because I do not nail him to my fantasies
or his fears,

May he not break and enter
his teenage daughter
small and closed as a shell.

May his small son's heart
not be blown away
like a white petal
by his dark storm.

That Girl

Through the hot kitchen window
stripped to the waist
legs parted, mouth wet with drink
the new workman was drilling
his eyes cemented to mine.

The butter from my toast dripped
onto my school tunic.
"You'd think he was having it off
instead of bloody drilling" said Yvonne.

"You watch him girl.
I've heard things.
There's some poor skinny bitch he keeps.
First he knocks her up
Now he knocks her about.
There's men for you"

Running to the bus-stop
I blocked out his body with my satchel.
"Heh! Blue eyes! Brown knickers!" he yelled.

After school
I saw her in that corner shop.
That girl.
They didn't have to point her out.

She was very thin.
She wore a long cardigan.
Yvonne whispered
that was to cover the bruises.

The shop went quiet.
The queue vanished -
I heard later she never had to queue
even near closing time.
The women just uneasily made way

Let her walk the plank of their guilt
her bruised face bent downwards
like a leper's bell.

Mrs. Sanders held out the drink and fags
— his —
the girl placed the exact money on the counter
a ritual without sound or touch

until she brushed against me.
I shivered.

All evening she kept brushing against me.
All evening I shivered
pleading "Talk to her, please talk to her"
to rows of frightened women crossing themselves
in their double beds.

In the morning
his wet mouth
shone through the glass
like a bloodstain.

For my two grandmothers

(1)

I carry the ghost of two grandmothers
soft as birdfeather, pale as old silk.
Dead Buba and dead Nanna,
two twin old embryos
alive alive O

(2)

Buba was shouting again in her other language,
talking about money and not being visited
and I was by the window
as far away as I could be
from her stained cups and saucers

pretending not to notice my father slip her money
which she presented to me
and I slipped back to him
and he returned to her

and through the yellowed lace curtains
I could see the old women rocking
on the other side of the street
rocking in rows through the large windows

and one who rocked so hard and high
her face looming and disappearing
I feared she would bring the whole street down
all the old women and their grandchildren hiding.

And their grandchildren hiding.

Yes.
It was there.
It must have been there.

The saturday afternoon at 2pm
(with arguments in the car all the way)
Buba shouting about Russian spies upstairs
her sons fleeing to Christian women.

I was as far away as I could be
from her matted hair and struggling mouth
and the window opposite was empty.
There was the swinging lightbulb and the flies
circling endlessly
but Buba saying the old woman was dead.

And the old woman was her
and she was dead
and I was the grandchild cowering in the corner

and Buba dead
with hardly any grey in her long black hair
hammers at the door of my dreams

and Buba mad
plaits into mattress
songs into curse
mouth wet with stale food

is ordering me to recognise her
is telling me she is mine.

(3)

Nanna grows weaker
I cover her rotting with mohair shawls
my friends talk quietly in the corner
I am praying she will not get up
I am praying she will not need the toilet
my kiss is a sleeping pill

Rockaby Nanna, she sleeps till they leave.
"Good" I say to her, kiss her, hug her.
I bring her cups of tea,
walk her to the toilet,
the room smells of stale earth.

I open windows, change cushions, shawls,
the wheelchair sneers a greasy grin,
but Nanna, Nanna,
smelling like a rotten banana

is a ghost who can pass through barbed wire
is a healer dressed in soiled clothes
whose body is leaving her
whose child-loving arms are folding together
into a last prayer

and Nanna in the oxygen tent
between the clean white sheets
dead and fresh and curled up like a foetus
I wrap, wrap, wrap inside me
and I rock up and down as she rocked me
and inside me she stirs, stirs.

(4)

I am a boarding house
a refugee camp
a slum
a temple

NO PRAYERS
says my landlady edict
in the English they cannot understand.

NO PRIVATE CEREMONIES NO FORBIDDEN LANGUAGES
NO CURSING SPITTING DEFECATING
ALL CROCKERY MUST BE STERILISED
ALL SOILED CLOTHING MUST BE BURNED.

There.
The fear.   •
PUT OUT THE FIRE

"Don't touch me" she said to her young lover,
"there is an old woman rotting between my legs
and I cannot wash the smell away".

I can't kiss Buba
her dripping mouth wants to drown me
but I can comb her matted hair

Oh but I can kiss the swollen hand of my Nanna

Nanna's angel eyes shine from a garbage heap
held together by crepe bandages.

(5)

My beautiful dead
soft as birdfeather, pale as old silk,
my old embryos.

The plaits break into air
the crepe bandage unwinds.

(6)

There's a pile of dry leaves singing prayers
I am pushing between two rotting trees.

VAL WINEYARD

I am 35 and divorced. I took the responsibility for the break-up and so I resent society's attitude towards me as someone who deserves to struggle because I choose to be independent. Apart from this, I live a happy and interesting life in North Wales with my two children, working sometimes as a freelance photographer and sometimes in a nine-to-five job — and writing poetry.

THE DIFFERENCE

When I stay in a friend's house
I straighten the bed and tidy the room
Before going downstairs to be
A Guest with a capital G.

But the man in my life
Thinks his friends are so pleased
To see him (and bed-making's prim)
That they'll tidy up after him.

'You don't *have* to do it,' he says.
'No-one makes you? Why feel guilty?
Be liberated from yourself!
Leave that duster on the shelf!'

'You women are all the same.
Where's my socks, I can't see in the dark.
Did you get the pills in case I'm ill?
Haven't you paid the electricity bill?'

WENDY HARRISON

Born in Nottinghamshire in 1953 but now lives and works as a teacher in Leicester. She studied English as one of her main subjects at college but did not attempt any serious writing of her own until about two years ago. Since then she has produced a number of poems, some of which reflect the feminist view explicitly, some implicitly. Most express the variety of feelings and conflicts experienced in the wide range of human relationships. Primarily her poems are about women and written to communicate with women.

conversation

it seems quite cold in
here though my face is
hot and my sleeves rolled
up then down again
your voice goes on i

cannot stop the theme
a precious one but
how shall i react
you did not hear my
words those years ago

on and on you go
oblivious of
all my feelings i
interrupt but on
goes the flow now i

almost shout but you
heard apparently
you had before your
eyes do not meet mine
at present because

a thousand garbled
messages hide my
old embarrassment
you care enough
to look away and as

it all teems out i
sense the oh so
familiar
release i am quite
used to our voices

soft and tender now
with tears unformed
but meant and i'd like to
touch but in the present
circumstances i

think i'll wait and in
they walk and we must
stop and start to eat
our cake instead we
pretend that we had

never spoken and
talking laughing safe
conversation where
the cheese was from but
as i catch your eye

there is no need to explain
as i slip into bed
i smile for
i have found you again

After a drink on a cold December night

Your rejection I can cope with
But not your arm
Around my shoulder
Afterwards.

NIGHT ENCOUNTER

I am not much taken to violence
But in this second I could kill you
For your lack of understanding
I despise the smile spreading over your face
What mess is inside to make you want to laugh?
Your seeming power as she loses speed
And cries to a world suffering from
Incurable deafness
The wood behind her splinters and she is aware
Of dirtying the coat her husband bought her
The first for years because with kids
You don't just get what you want
When you want it
As you blindly grab out I see you grit your teeth
Surely you don't need to try
To hold her steady, Strong Man
She sees her handbag fall and things tip out
Hysterically she thinks it was only cheap but
Still there were things inside
She wanted because library cards and pressed
Flowers off your wedding cake aren't easy
To replace
Money rattles on the gravel and stops in shock
But you don't see because you have her there
You even try a clumsy kiss
She feels your whiskers and remembers
Reading about things like this
Instructions telling you what to do
Even her grandmother carried a safety pin
At all times because you never know
And she'd tell her own too after this.

Your teeth are clenched, perhaps
They will break as you come
The groans you hear are not orgasmic
(Just in case you wondered)
They reveal stark fear
She feels your coat and shivers to think
What might be lurking in the wet grass
She might be dying for all she knows
The pain she bears and wonders when
The last bus goes

She always misses buses
Burdened too often with shopping, but not tonight
Just two bags of crisps to eat
While watching the T.V.
Maybe she'll not bother now
She realises her eyes are closed and he has gone
Her clothes are torn, some not here
Gathering her things she stands
Frightened though the worst is done she thinks
And feels uncomfortable, like
After giving birth
She almost slaps herself
At the comparison, but
What will they say at home?
She quietly weeps, resting her head
On a dirty post

The neighbours will laugh at her
Behind her back
Worse, she'd heard about a husband
Who'd left his wife, believing she'd
"Gone with someone else"
Well, after all, what's a man to think?
Hers was in the pub
And would be 'til it closed
She could hardly walk in now
Embarrassing him, so
She buttons her coat

P.C. Brown hums and drinks his tea
The night drags on
But on page three
He stops — it's for men you see
Young, normal hot blooded male
Another sees him looking
The point is made — he may turn over
No fools these people
They know that women who are raped
Probably ask for it . . .

ZOE FAIRBAIRNS

Daughter of Isabel. Born 1948. Educated by nuns but it didn't take. Lives in South-East London (well all right, Penge) trying to combine writing, feminism, teaching. Active in the Women's Research and Resources Centre and Spare Rib. *Co-author of* Tales I tell My Mother *(Journeyman, 1978). Author of* Benefits *(a futuristic novel) to be published by Virago, early 1980.*

the thing you'll like best

the thing you'll like best about going to bed with men
is their astonishing bigness.
even the little ones are bigger than us
yet they take care to fit.

the thing you'll like best about going to bed with men
is their pleasant politeness.
lips that would say ughnastyswampycunt
dip tastefully to kiss it.

the thing you'll like best about going to bed with men
is the featherbrush of hands like spanners
on anxious buttons; the way they don't
complain if service is long arriving.

the thing you'll like best about going to bed with men
is the vigour in the arms that hold you
not to imprison, not to lay waste,
but to encourage for some ordeal
where you'll prove you're not witch by drowning.

the thing you'll like best about going to bed with men
is the sense of being let off.

NO THANKS

A strange couple
with a man's name
have written to say it would give them great pleasure
to have me at the wedding of their daughter
to a one-time lover of mine.

No thanks.
But don't misunderstand.
It was years ago,
I also have another,
besides, it wouldn't matter
if the pair were strangers
ratting on a pledge;
or the groom my father,
or the bride my dearest friend.
The answer is the same —
I give the greatest pleasure
if I stay away from weddings.

(The only wedding I was ever good at
was one between consenting gays,
he with citizenship to bestow
upon she, who wished to stay in the country,
her lady being here.
I behaved well, I wore flowers,
if there'd been hymns I'd've sung.)

Normally, though, on these occasions,
I'm less than an asset.

When a sister I know has happily sensibly fucked her man for 16 months
glides down the aisle, white as a teacup,
my face cracks.

When father hauls the girl to the rail,
I lean to the mother on her second greatest day,
and, tender for the tears that give her away,
ask, 'Weren't you her parent too, then?
Did you do nothing?'

When the minister dares me to stop the proceedings
by freeing the wife from the attic,
I cry, 'There was an earlier commitment!
They said they would not do it!'
He says, 'O, everyone says that
when they're scared they won't be asked.'

And afterwards,
I fix my glittering eye upon the wedding-guests
('Wasn't she lovely?' 'No-one means it nowadays'
'It's nice to get together' 'Look at all the presents')
and rave of birds chained down to necks of sailors
till death do them part. 'Enjoy your gifts and moments
some of us do without.'

(You take my point
about staying away?)

No thanks.
I won't come just to the party either,
though what a nice suggestion!
I might just park my horse too close, you see,
and, pretending to dance, might scud across the floor
and scoop up bride and groom beneath each arm,
and three of us never be seen again.
I might not be able to stop myself.
So you see, if you don't mind . . .
or even if you do.

Alternatively, of course,
Zoe Fairbairns thanks you for your kind invitation
and deeply regrets a previous engagement.

OTHER PUBLICATIONS FROM ONLYWOMEN PRESS

BRAINCHILD—by Eve Croft £2.95 "Stylistically adventurous (yet in such a way as to make the writing more, not less, accessible) it describes the life of its bloody-minded, working class anti-heroine with so much aggression, honesty and wit that one ends up, not merely liking her, but taking on board her eternally defiant, remorseless view of the world." *City Limits*
"an East End version of The Women's Room . . . enjoyably scathing about middle-class radicals." *The Observer*

CACTUS—by Anna Wilson £2.25 "about two lesbian couples, one modern and managing to live in a society still fundamentally alien to them, one which broke up some twenty years before, mostly through social pressures. It is the least pretentious of books in terms of its subject matter (the women live in a small town, one keeps a greengrocer's shop) or of the statements it makes. This absence of artificial drama and the clear perceptions and skill of the author carry their own dignity." *The Guardian*

COMPULSORY HETEROSEXUALITY AND LESBIAN EXISTENCE—by Adrienne Rich 90p

WOMEN and HONOR: some notes on lying—by Adrienne Rich 35p

LOVE YOUR ENEMY?: the debate between heterosexual feminism and political lesbianism £1.75 a collection of letters and papers debating the place of sexuality in feminist theory and practice.

DOWN THERE—by Sophie Laws 75p A guide to self-examination of the vagina and cervix written and compiled by women for women.

HARD WORDS—by Caroline Griffin, Caroline Halliday and Sheila Shulman 40p Three lesbian feminists talk about the difficulties of their dialogue with heterosexual women.

NEW BOOKS COMING IN 1982

KINDLING—by Mary Dorcey. Lesbian feminist poetry bringing piercingly accurate insights from an Irish feminist.

An incisive feminist analysis of the sexual abuse of girls (as yet untitled) by the London Rape Crisis Centre collective.

RELATIVELY NORMA—by Anna Livia. A hilarious surrealist novel featuring keen cyclists, family life, lesbian feminists, Australian folkways and much more.

The first British Lesbian Anthology (as yet untitled) including fiction, theory, poems, photos and graphics.

Available through bookshops everywhere or directly from
Onlywomen Press, 38 Mount Pleasant, London WC1 XOAP